P9-CEI-002

MATIGNON HIGH SCHOOL
LIBRARY

Great Games
BY
Chess Prodigies

FRED REINFELD

Great Games BY Chess Prodigies

The Macmillan Company, New York
Collier-Macmillan Ltd., London

5707
794.1
R367G

Copyright © 1967 by The Macmillan Company
All rights reserved. No part of this book may be reproduced or transmitted in any form or by any means, electronic or mechanical, including photocopying, recording or by any information storage and retrieval system, without permission in writing from the Publisher.
Library of Congress Catalog Card Number: 67-10155
First Printing
The Macmillan Company, New York
Collier-Macmillan Canada Ltd., Toronto, Ontario
Printed in the United States of America

CONTENTS

Bobby Fischer 69

INTRODUCTION

CHESS IS a game which requires an enormous amount of aptitude, experience, study, determination. There is general agreement that chess is the most demanding of all games in these respects. Even a person completely ignorant of the game looks on the great masters with a feeling of awe, although some people prefer to mask this feeling with feeble quips that have passed into folklore.

Given the fantastically difficult requirements for mastery of chess, it is no wonder that only four authentic child prodigies have appeared in the history of the game. (I am using the term "authentic child prodigy" in a somewhat arbitrary sense. We are interested here in players who display an early phenomenal aptitude for the game *and then go on to become great masters in the days of their maturity.*)

Before studying (and enjoying) some of the fine games played by these prodigies, we should note that the conditions for achieving excellence in chess have become progressively more difficult as the general level of playing skill has steadily trended upward.

Thus, though I would be the last person to denigrate Paul Morphy's achievements, it must be admitted that his contemporaries were on the whole much weaker in ability than the modern-day masters. In this sense Capablanca's achievement was more remarkable, for after displaying early promise he distinguished himself in his early twenties by crushing a famous master (Frank Marshall) in a match, and then two years later by winning the San Sebastian tournament of 1911, one of the most formidable events of its kind.

Similarly, Sammy Reshevsky made good his early promise by winning the United States championship year after year against the most formidable opposition. Bobby Fischer's achievement in winning the United States championship at the age of fourteen against a very strong field leaves one at a loss for superlatives. We can at least say with certainty that this one achievement completely overshadows Morphy's victory against comparatively feeble opposition in the United States championship of 1857. In fact, I am willing to state categorically that there are at least fifty living masters each one of whom is capable of achieving an overwhelming plus score in a simultaneous exhibition against players of the caliber of Morphy's opponents of 1857.

So much for comparative playing levels, about which there will always be heated arguments among the partisans of this or that age. Meanwhile I invite the reader to revel in these delightful games, as he thinks of Paul Morphy sitting on a fat book in order to be able to queen his Pawns; of José Capablanca at the age of four ridiculing his father's inferior play; of Sammy Reshevsky playing in an international master tournament at the age of ten and defeating David Janowski, a grandmaster of international renown, in one of the most difficult games ever played in the history of tournament chess; of thirteen-year-old Bobby Fischer playing "the game of the century" against a leading American master.

Yes: these are games to arouse our wonderment, our gratitude, and, perhaps, our reverence for what the mind of man can achieve when it is directed toward constructive ends.

FRED REINFELD

Paul Morphy

THE CAREER of Paul Charles Morphy, who has fittingly been called "the pride and the sorrow of chess," reminds us poignantly of the fate of the Romantic poets, playwrights, novelists, artists, and musicians who were his contemporaries.

The early blossoming of Morphy's genius astounded the chess world, and his swift retirement at the height of his world fame was an equally sensational event. At the age of twenty-three he was through with competitive chess.

There is general agreement that Morphy learned to play at the age of ten. Whether he was taught by his father or learned by observation, we do not know. That Paul's progress was indeed rapid may be seen from the fact that he had no trouble beating his uncle, Ernest Morphy, acknowledged to be the best player in New Orleans.

Paul was born on June 23, 1837. He must therefore have started playing sometime in 1847. Two years later, under the date of October 31, 1849, his uncle wrote the following letter to the editor of *La Régence*, a French chess magazine:

> I send you herewith a game of chess played on the 28th instant between M. R.—— and the young Paul Morphy, my nephew, who is only twelve. The child has never opened a work on chess; he has learnt the game himself by following the *parties* [games] played between members of his family.

In the openings he makes the right moves as if by inspiration; and it is astonishing to note the precision of his calculations in the middle and end game. When seated before the chessboard, his face betrays no agitation even in the most critical positions; in such cases he generally whistles an air through his teeth and patiently seeks for the combination to get him out of trouble. Further, he plays three or four severe enough games every Sunday (the only day on which his father allows him to play) without showing the least fatigue.

Young Morphy grew up in an age when competitive chess was still in its infancy. The first international tournament had been held as recently as 1851, in London. Matches between great masters were still a novelty. Though chess had been played for over a thousand years, the theory of the game was still in a rudimentary state.

It is almost impossible for us to appreciate the sensation of young Morphy's emergence on the scene. He possessed to an astounding degree that uncanny quality of the child prodigy which consists in by-passing all the years of training and study that go into the making of a great practitioner of some art or science.

Morphy's ability, displayed at an amazingly early age, to defeat the best players of his time, was genuine and worthy of all praise. This was authentic genius at its most valid and solid level. Yet, without meaning to denigrate his achievements, the most significant aspect of his genius was something quite different: his intuitive discovery of one of the basic laws of chess. In early childhood young Paul had realized that proper play calls for rapid and consistent development of the pieces—a notion that had escaped every player up to that time.

This was Morphy's "secret weapon"—secret because his contemporaries failed to understand it. Nevertheless it was this weapon that toppled the recognized masters of his day, and it was this weapon that revolutionized chess. Once other players observed this technique, and came to appreciate it and adopt it in their own games, chess was on the way to becoming the game that we know in our own time.

1 *EVANS GAMBIT*

CASUAL GAME / NEW ORLEANS / 1849

This was the opening with which Morphy produced many of his brilliant games. Morphy immortalized the Evans, and the Evans immortalized him. This game was played against his uncle, Alonzo Morphy.

	White	*Black*
	P. MORPHY	A. MORPHY
1	P—K4	P—K4
2	N—KB3	N—QB3
3	B—B4	B—B4
4	P—QN4	....

White gives up a Pawn in order to gain time to form a powerful Pawn center and obtain a lead in development.

4	....	BxNP
5	P—B3	B—B4
6	P—Q4	PxP
7	PxP	B—N3
8	Castles	N—R4
9	B—Q3	P—Q4?

Though this looks promising, it has the drawback of opening up the game for White's pieces. What makes this particularly ominous is the fact that Black's pieces on the Queen-side are useless.

10	PxP	QxP
11	B—R3	....

Now Black cannot castle on the King-side.

11	....	B—K3

Hoping to castle on the other wing.

12	N—B3	Q—Q2
13	P—Q5!	....

A typical Morphy sacrifice which Black can hardly decline, for example 13 . . . B—N5; 14 R—K1 ch, K—Q1; 15 Q—K2 and White wins, for example 15 . . . N—R3; 16 B—N5 etc. or 15 . . . P—QR3; 16 B—B8!, P—KB3; 17 BxNP!

13	....	BxQP
14	NxB	QxN

DIAGRAM 1 Position after 14 . . . QxN

Black (A. MORPHY)

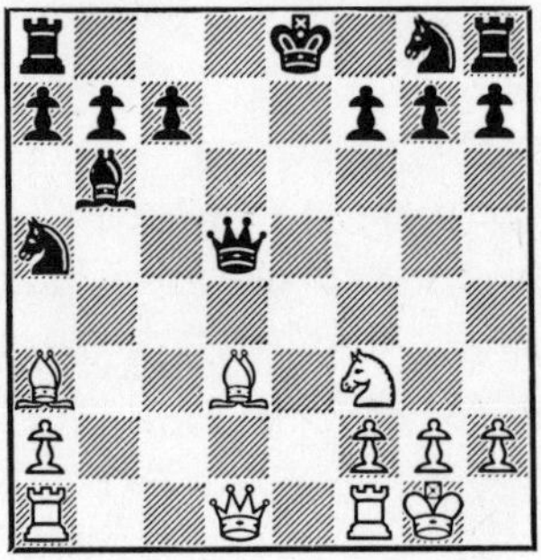

White (P. MORPHY)

15	B—N5 ch!?	....

Brilliant but not the simplest. There was an easy win with 15 R—K1 ch!, K—Q1; 16 B—N5! leaving Black defenseless.

15	....	QxB
16	R—K1 ch	N—K2
17	R—N1?	....

The right way was 17 RxN ch, K—B1; 18 R—N1, Q—R3; 19 Q—Q5 and wins.

17	....	Q—R3?

Now Black blunders. He could still put up a fight with 17 . . . Q—Q2!

18	RxN ch	K—B1
19	Q—Q5	Q—B5

He stops 20 QxBP mate, but White has another mate.

20	RxBP dbl ch	K—N1
21	R—B8 mate	

A very creditable game for a twelve-year-old.

2 *FRENCH DEFENSE*

CASUAL GAME / NEW ORLEANS / 1850

It is well known that Morphy was at home in the open games and had an equally strong dislike for the close games. The reason for this was doubtless that in open positions an advantage in development can be quickly turned to account, whereas in a close game it takes much more time to exploit a lead in development. Be that as it may, this is the only known example of Morphy's adopting the French Defense.

	White	*Black*
	McCONNELL	MORPHY
1	P—K4	P—K3
2	P—Q4	P—Q4
3	P—K5	P—QB4

An aggressive counter to White's aggressive-looking 3 P—K5. Black will get strong play on the Queen-side, particularly on the Queen Bishop file.

4	P—QB3	N—QB3
5	P—KB4?	. . . .

A fashionable move in those days, but it creates a weakness and loses time. Development with 5 N—B3 is in order.

5	....	Q—N3
6	N—B3	B—Q2
7	P—QR3?	....

Better 7 B—K2 etc.

7	....	N—R3!

Intending . . . N—B4 with added pressure on White's Queen Pawn.

8	P—QN4	PxQP
9	PxP	R—B1!

A typical Morphy situation: he has developed five pieces, White has developed only one.

10	B—N2	N—B4
11	Q—Q3	....

DIAGRAM 2 Position after 11 Q—Q3

Black (MORPHY)

White (MC CONNELL)

11	....	BxP ch!

The winning sacrifice.

12	PxB	NxNP
13	Q—Q2	....

Or 13 Q—Q1, N—B7 ch followed by 14 . . . QxB.

13	....	R—B7
14	Q—Q1	N—K6
	Resigns	

White's Queen is trapped!

3 *SCOTCH GAMBIT*

CASUAL GAME / MOBILE / 1855

This game is a very valuable one because of the move 5 . . . N—R3! It shows that even at this early stage—when Morphy was eighteen—he had already hit on the idea of developing pieces rapidly. The idea appears in an even more profound form than usual, for while we think of rapid development as an attacking device, Morphy applies it here for defensive purposes.

	White	*Black*
	MEEK	MORPHY
1	P—K4	P—K4
2	N—KB3	N—QB3
3	P—Q4	PxP
4	B—QB4	....

Very fashionable in those days, this move is nothing but a quaint antique in our own time.

4	....	B—B4
5	N—N5?	....

White loses time by moving an already developed piece. In those days it was customary to reply 5 . . . N—K4? likewise moving an already developed piece.

5	. . . .	N—R3!
6	NxBP	NxN
7	BxN ch	KxB
8	Q—R5 ch	P—KN3
9	QxB	P—Q3
10	Q—QN5	R—K1

Clearly, Morphy has the initiative.

11	Q—N3 ch	P—Q4
12	P—KB3	N—R4!

DIAGRAM 3 Position after 12 . . . N—R4!

Black (MORPHY)

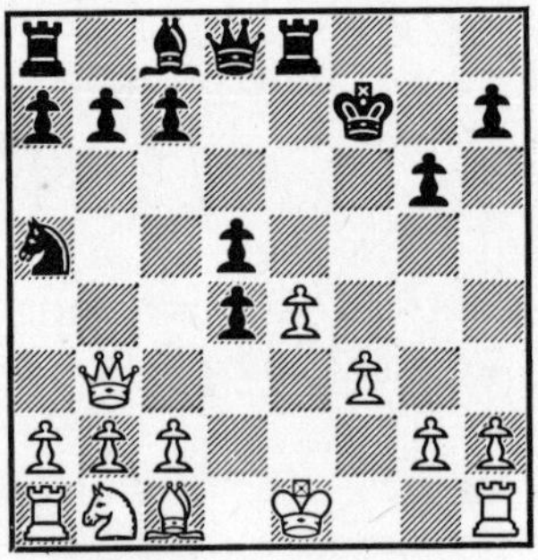

White (MEEK)

It is important to drive White's Queen off the diagonal. If now 13 Q—R4, PxP!; 14 QxN, PxP dis ch; 15 K—B1, P—N3!; 16 Q—KN5, PxP ch; 17 KxP, B—N2 ch—or 17 QxP, B—R3 ch—and Black wins quickly.

13	Q—Q3	PxP
14	PxP	Q—R5 ch
15	P—KN3	RxP ch

Black has a winning attack.

16	K—B2	Q—K2
17	N—Q2	R—K6
18	Q—N5	....

White must try to prevent . . . R—K7 ch—a point which is neatly exploited by Morphy.

18	....	P—B3!

So that if 19 QxN, then R—K7 ch and Black mates in two more moves.

19	Q—B1	B—R6!

The same theme: if 20 QxB, R—K7 ch; 21 K—B3, Q—K6 ch; 22 K—N4, Q—K3 ch; 23 K—R4, Q—B3 ch followed by mate in two.

20	Q—Q1	R—KB1!
21	N—B3	K—K1
	Resigns	

Morphy's play has been lucid and forceful.

4 *TWO KNIGHTS' DEFENSE (IN EFFECT)*

UNITED STATES CHAMPIONSHIP TOURNAMENT / 1857

The two-Rook sacrifice is one of the most elegant tactical themes in the attacking player's repertoire. Anderssen introduced this beautiful motif in 1851 in his famous "Immortal Game" with Kieseritzky, and that game was undoubtedly known to Morphy.

	White	*Black*
	LICHTENHEIN	MORPHY
1	P—K4	P—K4
2	N—KB3	N—QB3
3	P—Q4	PxP
4	B—QB4	N—B3
5	P—K5	P—Q4!

Much better than retreating the attacked Knight. If 6 PxN, PxB; 7 PxP, BxP and Black stands well.

6	B—QN5	N—K5
7	NxP	B—Q2

Notice how Morphy has already taken a lead in development.

8	NxN	PxN
9	B—Q3	B—QB4
10	BxN	Q—R5!

Always aggressive; Black threatens mate.

11	Q—K2	PxB

White should now castle. Many of Morphy's most brilliant combinations were made possible by his opponent's failure to castle in good time.

12	B—K3	B—KN5!

Deliberately provoking the following complications, as 13 Q—Q2 is refuted by 13 . . . R—Q1.

13	Q—B4	. . . .

DIAGRAM 4 Position after 13 Q—B4

Black (MORPHY)

White (LICHTENHEIN)

13	....	BxB

The intended continuation, for after 14 QxQBP ch, B—Q2!; 15 QxR ch, K—K2; 16 P—KN3, BxP ch!; 17 KxB, P—K6 ch; 18 K—K1 (if 18 K—N1, P—K7! wins), Q—QN5 ch; 19 P—B3, QxNP; 20 QxR, B—N5 mate follows.

14	P—KN3	Q—Q1!
15	PxB	Q—Q8 ch
16	K—B2	Q—B6 ch!

If now 17 K—K1, QxKP ch; 18 K—B1, B—R6 mate.

17	K—N1	B—R6

This forces mate.

18	QxQBP ch	K—B1
19	QxR ch	K—K2
	Resigns	

This game lasted only forty-five minutes!

5 *EVANS GAMBIT*

CASUAL GAME / NEW YORK / 1857

It is always fascinating to watch Morphy playing the defending side in a gambit. His opponent, who is presumably playing for attack, does not quite seem to know what it is all about. In very little time he is forced back relentlessly, bitterly mulling over his lost initiative.

	White	*Black*
	MARACHE	MORPHY
1	P—K4	P—K4
2	N—KB3	N—QB3
3	B—B4	B—B4
4	P—QN4	BxNP
5	P—B3	B—R4
6	P—Q4	PxP
7	P—K5	....

This premature advance is inferior to the usual 7 Castles.

7	....	P—Q4!
8	PxP *e.p.*	QxP
9	Castles	KN—K2

White's best is now 10 B—R3, Q—Q1; 11 PxP with not quite compensation for his Pawn. Instead, he embarks on a two-piece attack typical of the period.

10	N—N5?	Castles
11	B—Q3	....

The alternative 11 Q—R5 is simply answered by 11 . . . Q—N3.

11	....	B—B4!

Morphy gives up the exchange, getting three Pawns for it and maintaining his lead in development.

12	BxB	NxB
13	B—R3	Q—N3
14	BxR	QxN
15	B—R3	PxP
16	B—B1	Q—N3
17	B—B4	R—Q1
18	Q—B2	N/B3—Q5

DIAGRAM 5 Position after 18 . . . N/B3—Q5

Black (MORPHY)

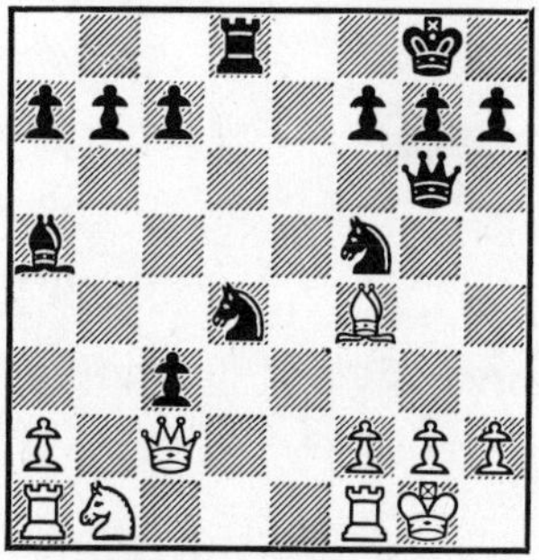

White (MARACHE)

The position is a gold mine of attacking threats.

For example, if White plays 19 Q—Q3, Black wins with the move actually played.

Or if 19 R—Q1, N—K6!; 20 QxQ, N—K7 ch; 21 K—R1, RxR mate.

Finally if 19 Q—R4, P—N4!; 20 QxB, N—K7 ch; 21 K—R1, NxB; 22 R—N1 (or 22 P—N3, Q—QB3 ch; 23 P—B3, QxP ch!; 24 RxQ, R—Q8 ch and mate next move), R—Q8!; 23 P—N3, Q—QB3 ch and mate next move.

19	Q—K4	N—KN6!
	Resigns	

If 20 QxQ, N/Q5—K7 mate. A sparkling finish to an instructive game, and a good example of Morphy's virtuosity with the Knights.

6 *FALKBEER COUNTER GAMBIT*

CASUAL GAME / NEW YORK / 1857

One of Morphy's favorite methods was the line-clearing Pawn sacrifice played on general principles. In the open games which Morphy loved, this type of sacrifice was bound to pay results, especially against weak opponents.

	White	*Black*
	SCHULTEN	MORPHY
1	P—K4	P—K4
2	P—KB4	P—Q4

Morphy has no intention of defending against the King's Gambit. Instead, he plays a counter gambit to snatch the attack.

3	KPxP	P—K5
4	N—QB3	N—KB3
5	P—Q3	B—QN5
6	B—Q2	....

White anticipates 6 . . . BxN or . . . PxP. Instead:

6	....	P—K6!
7	BxP	Castles

Now Morphy intends to utilize the newly opened King file by playing the pinning move . . . R—K1.

8	B—Q2	BxN!
9	PxB	R—K1 ch
10	B—K2	B—N5
11	P—B4?	....

White would be better off with 11 K—B2, getting out of the pin.

11	....	P—B3!
12	PxP	NxP

Morphy has the attacking position he wants, for example 13 B—B3, N—Q5; 14 BxN, QxB; 15 N—B3, BxN; 16 PxB, N—R4; 17 R—KB1, NxP; 18 R—B2, R—K2 followed by . . . QR—K1 and wins.

13	K—B1	RxB!
14	NxR	N—Q5
15	Q—N1	BxN ch
16	K—B2	N—N5 ch

With some pretty ideas: 17 K—N3, N—B4 ch; 18 K—R3, Q—R5 mate or 17 K—K1, Q—R5 ch; 18 P—N3, R—K1!; 19 PxQ, N—B6 mate.

17	K—N1	....

DIAGRAM 6 Position after 17 K—N1

Black (MORPHY)

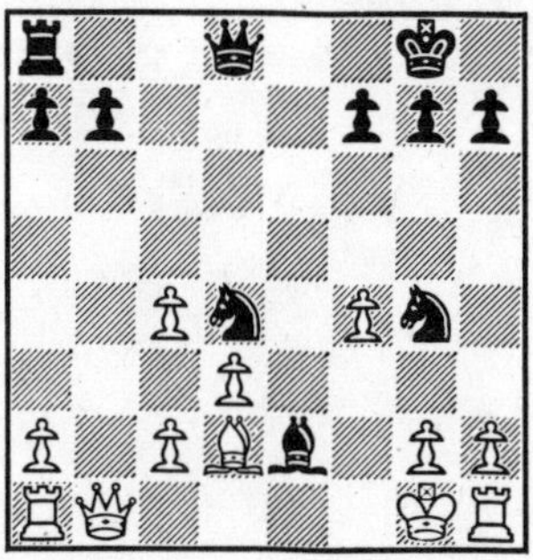

White (SCHULTEN)

17	....	N—B6 ch!
18	PxN	Q—Q5 ch
19	K—N2	Q—B7 ch

20	K—R3	QxBP ch
21	K—R4	N—K6
22	R—N1	N—B4 ch
23	K—N5	Q—R4 mate

7 *PHILIDOR'S DEFENSE*

MORPHY PLAYS BLINDFOLD / PARIS / 1858

This game was played against the Duke of Brunswick and Count Isouard during an intermission of a performance of Rossini's *Barber of Seville* at the Paris Opera. It conveys the essence of Morphy's classic style better than any other game, reminding us that "a thing of beauty is a joy forever."

	White	*Black*
	MORPHY	ALLIES
1	P—K4	P—K4
2	N—KB3	P—Q3

A favorite method in those days of avoiding the dreaded Evans (2 . . . N—QB3; 3 B—B4, B—B4; 4 P—QN4 etc.).

3	P—Q4	B—N5?
4	PxP	BxN

The alternative 4 . . . PxP loses a Pawn by 5 QxQ ch, KxQ; 6 NxP etc.

5	QxB	PxP
6	B—QB4	. . . .

Development with a mate threat: what could be sweeter?

6	. . . .	N—KB3

The alternative 6 . . . Q—B3; 7 Q—QN3, P—QN3; 8 N—B3, P—B3 is not inviting.

7	Q—QN3!	Q—K2

Hoping for 8 QxP, Q—N5 ch and Black exchanges Queens. But Morphy is not satisfied with a picayune continuation.

8	N—B3	P—B3
9	B—KN5	P—N4
10	NxP!	PxN
11	BxNP ch	QN—Q2
12	Castles/Q	....

Now Black is subjected to two powerful pins.

12	....	R—Q1
13	RxN!	RxR
14	R—Q1	Q—K3

Hopeless, but there is no good move.

DIAGRAM 7 Position after 14 . . . Q—K3

Black (ALLIES)

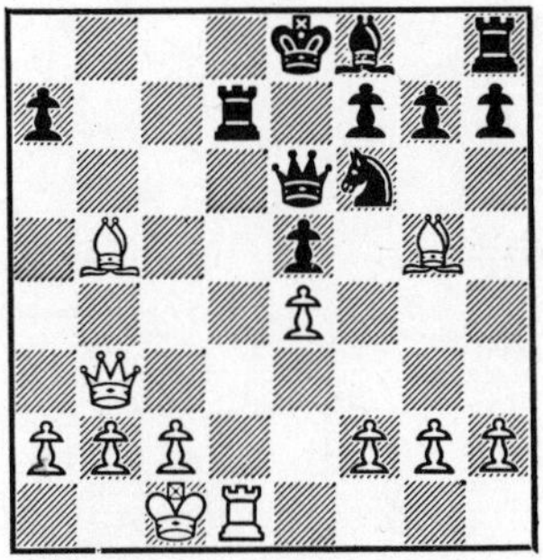

White (MORPHY)

Now White has a simple win with 15 BxN, but he finds something much more drastic.

15	BxR ch	NxB
16	Q—N8 ch!	NxQ
17	R—Q8 mate	

This game has been described as "a Damascus blade cutting a silk cushion."

8 *EVANS GAMBIT*

SIMULTANEOUS BLINDFOLD EXHIBITION / NEW ORLEANS / 1858

No other game reveals so well as this one Morphy's genius for the open game. It is indeed one of the most impressive masterpieces in the annals of blindfold play.

	White	*Black*
	MORPHY	AMATEUR
1	P—K4	P—K4
2	N—KB3	N—QB3
3	B—B4	B—B4
4	P—QN4	BxNP
5	P—B3	B—R4
6	P—Q4	PxP
7	Castles	PxP

The famous Compromised Defense, so called because in Morphy's day it was felt that the Pawn captures were more than Black could stand. In later years, however, the analysts concluded that the defense was playable.

8	B—R3	P—Q3
9	Q—N3	N—R3
10	NxP	BxN

Not liking the possibility of N—Q5; but now White has two powerful Bishops against Bishop and Knight.

11	QxB	Castles
12	QR—Q1	....

Threatens P—K5.

12	....	N—KN5
13	P—R3	KN—K4
14	NxN	NxN

Black forces White's King Bishop off his diagonal, as 15 B—N3 is met by 15 . . . B—K3.

15	B—K2	P—KB4?

The player with inferior development should never open up the position. The right way was 15 . . . P—KB3.

16	P—B4!	N—B3
17	B—B4 ch	K—R1
18	B—N2	Q—K2
19	QR—K1	R—B3

If 19 . . . PxP; 20 RxP! with a winning position. While Morphy monopolizes the open lines, Black has several pieces that are useless.

20	PxP	Q—B1

DIAGRAM 8 Position after 20 . . . Q—B1

Black (AMATEUR)

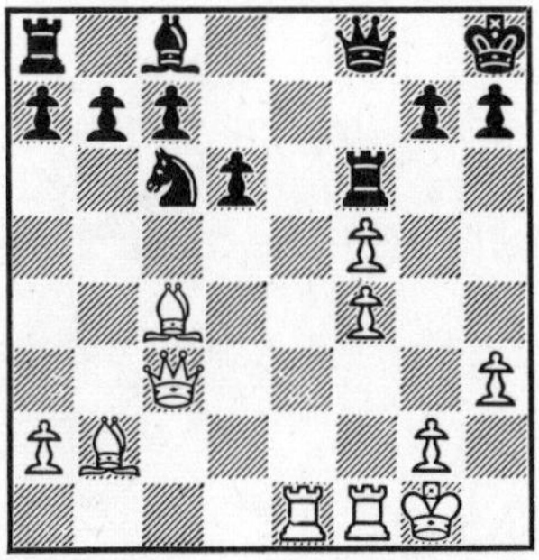

White (MORPHY)

21	R—K8!!	QxR
22	QxR!	Q—K2

Now the easiest win is 23 QxQ, NxQ; 24 R—K1!, N—N1; 25 R—K8. But the blindfold player "sees" a more spectacular line.

23	QxP ch!	QxQ
24	P—B6!	QxP ch

Or 24 . . . Q—B1; 25 P—B7 dis ch, N—K4; 26 PxN, P—KR4; 27 P—K6 dis ch, K—R2; 28 B—Q3 ch, K—R3; 29 R—B6 ch, K—N4; 30 R—N6 ch, K—B5; 31 K—B2! leading to mate!

25	KxQ	BxP ch

If 25 . . . P—KR4; 26 P—B7 dis ch wins at once.

26	KxB	P—KR4
27	R—KN1	Resigns

A gem of a game.

9 *TWO KNIGHTS' DEFENSE*

SIMULTANEOUS BLINDFOLD EXHIBITION / NEW ORLEANS / 1858

Morphy's sharp attacking play sparkles with an almost sadistic relish. Black's King is hounded to death at QN3 after a series of delightful sacrifices.

	White	*Black*
	MORPHY	AMATEUR
1	P—K4	P—K4
2	N—KB3	N—QB3
3	B—B4	N—B3
4	P—Q4	PxP
5	N—N5	. . . .

Morphy takes liberties with a weak opponent.

5	....	P—Q4!
6	PxP	NxP?

Here 6 . . . Q—K2 ch! assures equality.

7	Castles	....

Black is in trouble. Consider these possibilities: if 7 . . . B—K3; 8 R—K1, then 8 . . . B—K2; 9 RxB!, PxR; 10 NxKP, Q—Q2; 11 Q—R5 ch, P—KN3; 12 QxN. Or 8 . . . Q—Q2; 9 NxBP!, KxN; 10 Q—B3 ch, K—N1 (if 10 . . . K—N3; 11 RxB ch!, QxR; 12 B—Q3 ch forcing mate); 11 RxB! and wins.

7	....	B—K2
8	NxBP!	....

A form of the Fegatello ("fried liver") Attack, with which Morphy scored some pretty wins.

8	....	KxN
9	Q—B3 ch	K—K3
10	N—B3!!	PxN
11	R—K1 ch	N—K4
12	B—B4	B—B3
13	BxN	BxB

DIAGRAM 9 Position after 13 . . . BxB

Black (AMATEUR)

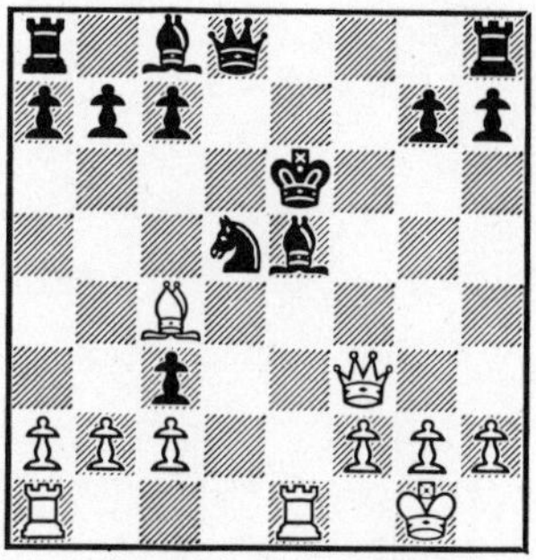

White (MORPHY)

14	RxB ch!	....

One forcing move after another. The attack is sheer delight.

14	....	KxR
15	R—K1 ch	K—Q5

Forced.

16	BxN	R—K1

Not 16 . . . QxB; 17 QxP mate! Or 16 . . . PxP; 17 R—K4 ch!, K—B4; 18 Q—QR3 ch!, KxB; 19 Q—Q3 ch, K—B4; 20 R—QB4 ch and mate in two.

17	Q—Q3 ch	K—B4
18	P—QN ch!!	KxP

If 18 . . . K—N3; 19 Q—Q4 ch, K—R3; 20 Q—QB4 ch and White mates in two.

19	Q—Q4 ch	K—R4

After 19 . . . K—R6 White would apply the same mating method. Now Morphy announced mate in four:

20	QxBP ch	K—R5
21	Q—QN3 ch	K—R4
22	Q—QR3 ch	K—N3
23	R—N1 mate	

A typical Morphy game.

José R. Capablanca

CHILD PRODIGIES have a way of not fulfilling the promise of their early spectacular achievements. This was not true of Capablanca, who lived to become a World Champion. His strong point, both as a child prodigy and as a mature master, was an instinctive grasp of every position and a quick realization of what the proper course should be. Other masters, even the greatest, had to struggle and toil for their best moves; to Capablanca this process seemed child's play.

In *My Chess Career* he left us an entertaining account of his introduction to the game:

> I was born in Havana, the capital of the island of Cuba, the 19th of November, 1888. I was not yet five years old when by accident I came into my father's private office and found him playing with another gentleman. I had never seen a game of chess before; the pieces interested me, and I went the next day to see them play again. The third day, as I looked on, my father, a very poor beginner, moved a Knight from a white square to another white square. His opponent, apparently not a better player, did not notice it. My father won, and I proceeded to call him a cheat and to laugh. After a little wrangle, during which I was nearly put out of the room, I showed my father what he had done. He asked me how and what I knew about chess. I answered that I could

beat him; he said that that was impossible, considering that I could not even set the pieces correctly. We tried conclusions, and I won. That was my beginning. A few days after, my father took me to the Havana Chess Club, where the strongest players found it impossible to give me a Queen. About that time the Russian master, Taubenhaus, visited Havana, and he declared it beyond him to give me such odds. Later, in Paris, in 1911, Mr. Taubenhaus would often say, "I am the only living master who has given Mr. Capablanca a Queen."

Young José continued to improve, still without devoting any systematic study to the game, and at the age of twelve he played a match for the championship of Cuba. Though heavily handicapped by his lack of routine and experience, the youngster won the contest in impressive style.

Several years later the young man came to the United States to study at Columbia University. His skill at simultaneous play earned him such a reputation that he was matched to play against Frank J. Marshall, then at the height of his powers.

Even Capablanca's strongest admirers could not have expected anything more of him than a creditable defeat at the hands of his world-famous opponent. Instead, the result was thoroughly unexpected. Capablanca seized the lead at the very start and crushed Marshall mercilessly. The final score was 8–1 in the younger man's favor.

The overwhelming nature of this score is a good indication that the Cuban's victory was no fluke. This impression is reinforced by the games themselves, which show Capablanca as a mature master in all respects, aside from his timorous handling of the openings.

Two years later Capablanca went on to an even more remarkable success by winning the San Sebastian tournament of 1911, one of the strongest international tournaments ever held. Throughout the chess world he was recognized as a child prodigy who had made good. His defeat of Emanuel Lasker ten years later for the world championship was so widely expected that it came in the nature of anticlimax.

10 *PETROFF'S DEFENSE*

HAVANA / 1893

[*Remove White's Queen*]

Although a game at these stupendous odds is of no interest on its merits, it takes on enormous value when we learn that little José played it at the age of four years and ten months! Black's moves offer considerable evidence of a grasp of chess that is simply phenomenal in a little child.

	White	*Black*
	IGLESIAS	CAPABLANCA
1	P—K4	P—K4
2	N—KB3	N—KB3
3	NxP	NxP
4	P—Q4	P—Q3
5	N—KB3	B—K2
6	B—Q3	N—KB3
7	P—B4	Castles
8	N—B3	N—B3

Black has already made it clear that he is aware of the importance of developing his pieces. This is a hint that the odds are too great.

9	P—QR3	P—QR3
10	B—Q2	P—QN3
11	Castles/Q	B—Q2
12	K—N1	N—QR4
13	R—QB1	N—N6
14	R—B2	P—B4
15	P—Q5	R—K1
16	P—KR4	P—QN4!

The huge odds make it impossible for White to proceed in any constructive manner. Usually the outcome of such games is determined by blunders on the part of the odds-receiver—but here he makes no blunders.

DIAGRAM 10 Position after 16 . . . P—QN4!

Black (CAPABLANCA)

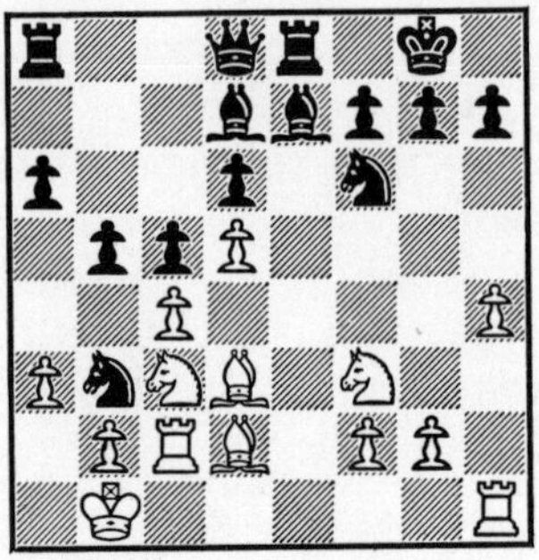

White (IGLESIAS)

17	P—N4	N—Q5

There is no objection to capturing the King Knight Pawn at once, but Black's last move introduces some simplification—always bad for the odds-giver.

18	NxN	PxN
19	N—K4	PxP
20	NxN ch	BxN
21	BxBP	BxNP

With the threat of 22 . . . B—B4.

22	B—Q3	B—B6
23	R—R3	BxQP
24	P—R5	B—K3
25	R—N3	P—N3
26	P—B4	B—R5
27	R—N1	K—R1
28	P—B5	BxP
29	BxB	PxB
30	B—R6	KR—N1

Parrying the threat of B—N7 ch etc.

31	R/B2—N2	RxR
32	RxR	Q—B3

Or simply 32 . . . B—B3.

33	B—N7 ch	QxB
34	RxQ	KxR
35	K—B2	K—B3
36	K—Q3	K—K4
37	P—R6	P—B5
38	K—K2	K—K5
	Resigns	

And none too soon. An amazing game for a four-year-old.

11 *HAMPPE-ALLGAIER GAMBIT*

MATCH / 1900

The opening here is typical of child-prodigy chess. The more experienced player chooses tricky lines in the hope of trapping his untutored young opponent. But the prodigy has a way of sure-footedly avoiding the pitfalls.

	White	*Black*
	J. CORZO	CAPABLANCA
1	P—K4	P—K4
2	N—QB3	N—QB3
3	P—B4	PxP
4	N—B3	P—KN4
5	P—KR4	P—N5
6	N—KN5!?	P—KR3
7	NxP	KxN

White has chosen a complicated and basically unsound sacrificial line in the hope of bewildering his young opponent.

8	P—Q4	P—Q4
9	PxP	Q—K2 ch
10	K—B2	P—N6 ch
11	K—N1	....

White expects 11 . . . N—N1; 12 B—B4 (threatens P—Q6 dis ch), K—N2; 13 BxP with a tremendous attack.

DIAGRAM 11 Position after 11 K—N1

Black (CAPABLANCA)

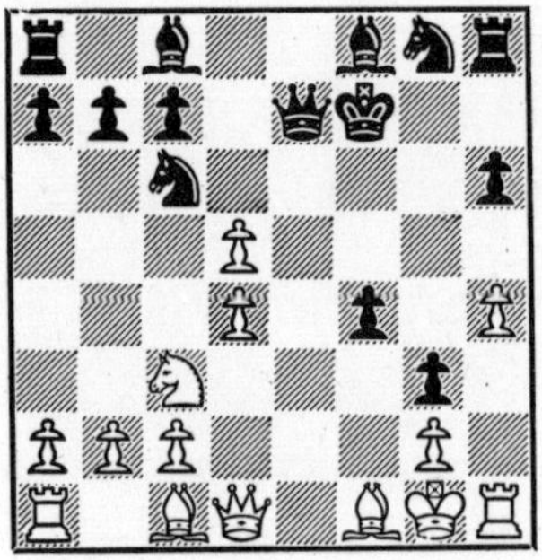

White (CORZO)

11	....	NxP!!

Very fine. Black beats back the attack and forces a favorable ending.

12	QxN	Q—B4

The point: if 13 QxQ??, BxQ ch; 14 B—K3, BxB mate!

13	N—K2	Q—N3!

With the terrible threat of . . . B—QB4. White must exchange Queens.

14	QxQ	RPxQ
15	N—Q4	B—QB4
16	P—B3	R—R5!

Threatens 17 . . . RxN!

17	B—K2	. . . .

Or 17 P—N4, RxNP!

17	. . . .	BxN ch
18	PxB	RxQP
19	P—N3	N—B3
20	B—N2	R—Q7

He avoids 20 . . . RxP?; 21 B—B4.

21	B—R5 ch	NxB!
22	BxR	P—B6!
23	PxP	N—B5
24	B—K5	. . . .

Or 24 R—K1, B—R6!; 25 B—K5 (if 25 RxB, NxR ch and mate next move), R—KN7 ch; 26 K—B1, R—KB7 dbl ch; 27 K—N1, R—B8 ch! (or 27 . . . N—K7 ch; 28 RxN, R—B8 mate); 28 RxR, N—K7 mate.

24	. . . .	R—KN7 ch
25	K—B1	R—KB7 ch
26	K—K1	N—Q6 ch
	Resigns	

After 27 K—Q1, NxB, Black wins quickly. A remarkable game.

12 *QUEEN'S PAWN OPENING*

MATCH / 1900

White's play in the middle game and end game phase is incredible. His moves could not be improved on by a mature master.

	White	*Black*
	CAPABLANCA	J. CORZO
1	P—Q4	P—Q4
2	N—KB3	P—QB4
3	P—K3	N—QB3
4	P—QN3	P—K3
5	B—N2	N—B3
6	QN—Q2	PxP

This superficial move gives White a strong point for his King Knight at K5.

7	PxP	B—Q3
8	B—Q3	Castles
9	Castles	N—KR4
10	P—N3	P—B4
11	N—K5	N—B3
12	P—KB4	BxN
13	BPxB	N—KN5?

The Knight is destined to be useless, hence 13 . . . N—K5 was preferable.

14	Q—K2	Q—N3
15	N—B3	B—Q2

Here . . . N—QN5 was more timely.

16	P—QR3	K—R1
17	P—R3	N—R3
18	Q—B2	N—B2
19	K—N2	P—N4

This makes Black vulnerable on the long diagonal. The weakness is beautifully exploited by White.

20	P—KN4!	N—K2

On 20 . . . P—B5 White has a powerful reply in 21 P—KR4!

21	Q—K3	R—KN1
22	QR—K1	N—N3
23	PxP!	N—B5 ch
24	K—R2	NxB
25	QxN	PxP
26	P—B4!	....

White has completed his masterly preparations for forcing the long diagonal open.

26	....	Q—K3
27	PxP	QxP
28	P—K6!	B—N4

Not 28 . . . BxP; 29 RxB!, QxR; 30 P—Q5 dis ch winning the Queen.

DIAGRAM 12 Position after 28 . . . B—N4

Black (CORZO)

White (CAPABLANCA)

29	QxB!!?	....

Very pretty, though there is a quicker win with 29 Q—Q2!, BxR; 30 PxN, QxBP (if 30 . . . QxN; 31 P—Q5 dis ch!, R—N2; 32 R—K8 ch forces mate); 31 P—Q5 dis ch, R—N2; 32 NxP, Q—N3; 33 R—K7, QR—KN1; 34 N—B7 ch and Black can resign.

29	....	QxQ
30	P—Q5 dis ch	R—N2
31	PxN	P—KR3

The alternative 31 . . . R—KB1 will not do because of 32 N—Q4, QxQP; 33 R—K8, QxBP; 34 RxR ch, QxR; 35 NxP etc.

32	N—Q4	QxR

Black resigns to the inevitable. After 32 . . . Q—Q2; 33 NxP, QxBP; 34 BxR ch, K—R2; 35 R—K7 his situation is hopeless.

33	RxQ	RxP
34	RxP	RxR
35	NxR dis ch	K—R2
36	N—K7!	....

Young Capablanca handles the whole ending with fine technique. Preparing to queen his passed Queen Pawn he first blocks off Black's King.

36	....	R—KB1
37	K—N2	P—KR4
38	P—Q6	P—N5
39	PxP	PxP
40	B—K5	K—R3
41	P—Q7	R—Q1
42	N—N8 ch!	RxN

No better is 42 . . . K—N3; 43 N—B6, K—B2; 44 B—B7 and Black's Rook must go.

43	B—B6	K—N3
44	P—Q8/Q	RxQ
45	BxR	P—N4
46	K—B2	K—B4
47	K—K3	K—K4
48	K—Q3	K—Q4
49	K—B3	P—N6
50	B—R4	P—N7

51	B—B2	P—R4
52	P—N4!	....

If now 52 . . . P—R5; 53 K—Q3, K—K4; 54 B—N1, K—Q4; 55 B—Q4, K—K3; 56 K—K4, K—Q3; 57 B—K5 ch, K—K3; 58 B—R2, K—Q2; 59 K—Q5 and wins. There are various ways of carrying out this maneuver.

52	....	K—K5

Hoping for 53 PxP?, K—Q4 and White cannot win because his Rook Pawns have to queen on a square of the "wrong color."

53	B—N6	K—Q4
54	K—Q3	K—B3
55	B—N1	K—Q4
56	B—R2!	K—B3
57	K—Q4	P—R5
58	K—K5	K—N3

Black's King must continue to give ground.

59	K—Q5	K—R3

Black's last hope: 60 K—B6??, P—N8/Q!; 61 BxQ—stalemate!

60	K—B5!	Resigns

Both Black's Queen-side Pawns must fall. A most impressive achievement.

13 *FRENCH DEFENSE*

HAVANA / 1902

Again the child prodigy starts out with a colorless opening and then reveals his skill in the middle game and endgame.

	White	*Black*
	E. CORZO	CAPABLANCA
1	P—K4	P—K3
2	P—Q4	P—Q4
3	N—QB3	PxP
4	NxP	B—Q2
5	N—KB3	B—B3
6	B—Q3	N—Q2

Black has adopted a passive defense which gives him a constricted position.

7	Castles	KN—B3
8	B—KN5	....

As White has the freer game he should avoid exchanges (8 N—N3).

8	....	B—K2
9	NxN ch	BxN
10	B—K3	Castles
11	P—B3	P—QN3
12	Q—B2	K—R1

A trap. Black offers his opponent the opportunity of giving up a piece for three Pawns, but this would be fatal: 13 BxP?, BxN!; 14 PxB, P—KN3; 15 BxP, PxB; 16 QxP?, R—KN1 winning the Queen.

13	N—Q2	R—K1

Again offering White the same opportunity, which can be ventured safely here. However, Black accurately foresees that his extra piece will be more useful than White's extra Pawns.

14	BxP	P—N3
15	BxP	PxB
16	QxP	Q—K2

Not 16 . . . K—N1??; 17 Q—R6 mate.

17	P—KB4	Q—R2
18	QxQ ch	KxQ
19	N—B3	. . . .

The alternative 19 P—KN4 was more forceful. Now Black cleverly seizes the initiative.

19	. . . .	R—KN1
20	QR—K1	R—N3
21	B—Q2	B—Q4
22	P—QN3	R—KB1
23	K—R1	P—B4

Black is steadily gaining ground for his pieces.

24	PxP	NxP
25	P—B4	B—QR1
26	B—N4	R/B1—KN1
27	BxN	. . . .

His best chance was 27 R—K2. But White can hardly be blamed for failing to foresee Black's magnificent reply.

DIAGRAM 13 Position after 27 BxN

Black (CAPABLANCA)

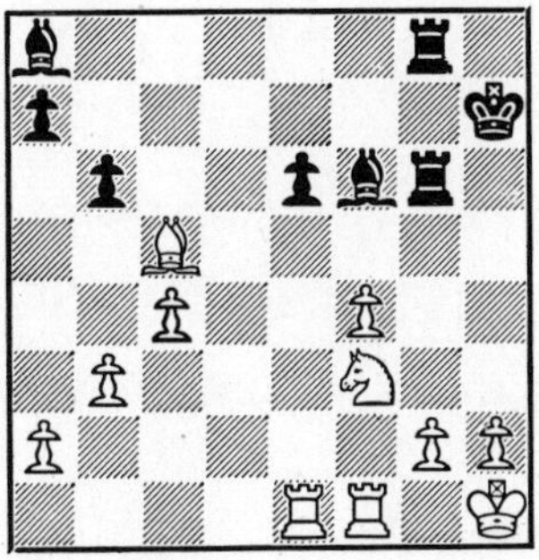

White (CORZO)

27	....	RxP!!

White cannot retreat by means of 28 B—R3 or B—N4, as the reply 28 . . . R—N8 ch!! is deadly.

Nor will 28 B—N1 do (28 . . . RxB ch!).

Finally, if 28 RxP, PxB; 29 RxB, BxN, then mate follows (or 29 R—K3, B—Q5; 30 R—Q3, R—N8 ch and mate next move).

28	B—K3	B—R5!

Threatening 29 . . . BxR, as White will be unable to retake.

29	R—Q1	B—B7!

Very pretty: the Bishop cannot be captured either way.

30	R—Q7 ch	K—R3
31	R—Q5	....

White must close the diagonal as Black is threatening mate in two, beginning with . . . R—N8 ch.

31	....	BxB
32	N—N5	R/N7xN!
33	PxN ch	RxP
34	R—B6 ch	K—R4
35	RxP	BxR ch
	Resigns	

For 36 PxB is answered by 36 . . . R—N8 mate. A remarkably sophisticated game.

14 *KING'S GAMBIT*

CASUAL GAME / NEW YORK / 1906

After a slow start, Black works up a terrific attack, thanks to White's helpful cooperation.

	White	*Black*
	RAUBITSCHECK	CAPABLANCA
1	P—K4	P—K4
2	P—KB4	PxP
3	N—KB3	P—KN4
4	B—B4	B—N2
5	P—KR4	P—KR3

An old-fashioned form of the gambit which leaves Black with a fair game.

6	P—Q4	N—QB3
7	P—B3	P—Q3
8	Castles	Q—K2
9	Q—N3	N—Q1

In order to be able to develop his Queen Bishop. At the same time, Black allows White to win two Pawns, coming out a Pawn ahead—but only at the cost of opening up attacking lines for Black.

10	PxP	PxP
11	Q—N5 ch	B—Q2
12	QxKNP	B—KB3
13	QxP	N—K3
14	BxN	....

White parts too readily with his more effective Bishop; 14 Q—K3 would have been better.

14	....	BxB
15	P—K5	....

Opening up good prospects for Black's Queen Bishop. Simple development was in order.

15	....	PxP
16	NxP	....

And here 16 PxP would be better. Aided by White's errors of omission and commission, Black now works up a terrific attack.

16	....	Castles
17	N—R3	R—R5
18	Q—N3	BxN
19	QxB	R—Q4
20	Q—N7?	R—N5
21	Q—R7	N—B3!

Capablanca is planning a beautiful combination.

22	Q—R8 ch	R—Q1!
23	QxN	....

DIAGRAM 14 Position after 23 QxN

Black (CAPABLANCA)

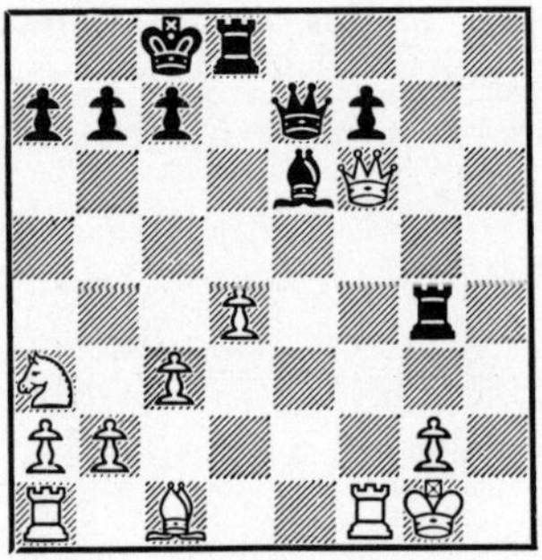

White (RAUBITSCHECK)

23	....	QR—N1!

The fitting sequel to the previous sacrifice. If now 24 QxQ, RxP ch; 25 K—R1, B—Q4!; 26 Q—K5, R/N7—N2 dis ch; 27 QxB, R—R1 ch and mate next move.

24	R—B2	RxP ch
25	K—B1	B—B5 ch!
26	NxB	R—N8 mate

Very pretty play against a weak opponent.

15 *RUY LOPEZ*

MATCH / 1909

Though this game was played at the beginning of Capablanca's career as a master, it ranks as one of the best he ever played.

	White	*Black*
	CAPABLANCA	MARSHALL
1	P—K4	P—K4
2	N—KB3	N—QB3
3	B—N5	P—Q3
4	P—B3	....

Capablanca's ignorance of opening theory leads him to play too conservatively. The usual move is 4 P—Q4.

4	....	B—N5

This maneuver with the Bishop turns out rather unfortunately. Simple and good is 4 . . . P—KN3; 5 P—Q4, B—Q2 followed by . . . B—N2.

5	P—Q3	B—K2
6	QN—Q2	N—B3
7	Castles	Castles
8	R—K1	P—KR3

Thanks to White's colorless play, Black can free himself with 8 . . . P—QR3; 9 B—R4, P—QN4; 10 B—N3, P—Q4.

9	N—B1	N—R2
10	N—K3	B—R4
11	P—KN4	B—N3
12	N—B5	P—KR4?

Black can still obtain fair prospects with 12 . . . N—N4; 13 K—N2, NxN; 14 QxN, B—N4.

13	P—KR3	PxP?

In a sense this is the losing move, opening the King Rook file for White.

14	PxP	B—N4
15	NxB	NxN
16	K—N2	P—Q4
17	Q—K2	R—K1
18	R—R1	....

White intends to double Rooks on the open file.

18	....	R—K3

Black hopes for 19 BxKN, QxB; 20 PxP, BxN; 21 PxR, BxNP with good attacking chances in return for the exchange.

19	Q—K3!	P—B3

If instead 19 . . . N—R2; 20 Q—R3 threatening 21 N—R4 with powerful effect.

20	B—R4!	N—K2
21	B—N3!	....

This Bishop's pressure will be felt right down to KN8.

21	....	P—B3
22	Q—N3	P—R4
23	P—R4	....

He maintains his King Bishop at its effective post by preventing . . . P—R5.

23	....	N—B2
24	B—K3	P—N3
25	R—R4	K—B1
26	QR—R1	N—N1
27	Q—B3!	....

Very fine. This puts additional pressure on Black's Queen Pawn, which cannot be defended by . . . R—Q3. If Black tries to solve the problem by 27 . . . PxP there follows 28 PxP, R—K1; 29 Q—R3 intending 30 R—R8! and White's attack crashes through.

27	....	BxN
28	NPxB	R—Q3
29	Q—R5	R—R2
30	Q—N6	....

With the powerful threat of 31 R—R7.

If Black tries to drive White's Queen away with 30 . . . N—K2 there is a neat win with 31 R—R8 ch!, NxR; 32 RxN ch, N—N1; 33 Q—R7, K—B2; 34 BxNP! etc.

30	....	N/B2—R3

A futile attempt to dam the flood.

DIAGRAM 15 Position after 30 . . . N/B2—R3

Black (MARSHALL)

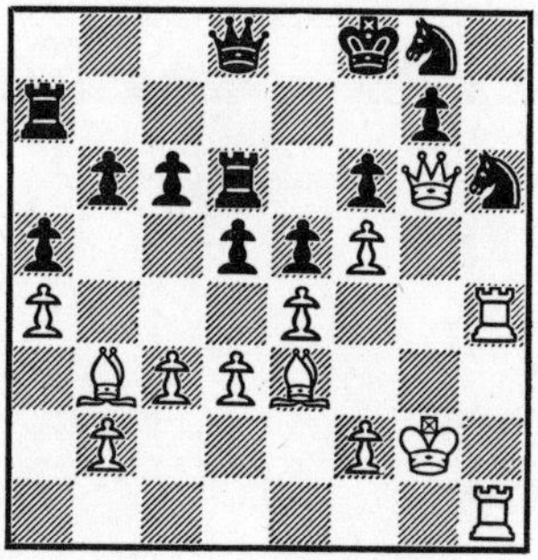

White (CAPABLANCA)

31	RxN!	PxR

Or 31 . . . NxR; 32 BxN and White wins easily.

32	BxP ch	K—K2

If 32 . . . NxB; 33 RxN and Black has no defense.

33	Q—N7 ch	K—K1
34	QxN ch	K—Q2

Now comes a fine finish.

35	Q—R7 ch!	Q—K2
36	B—B8!	QxQ
37	RxQ ch	K—K1
38	RxR	Resigns

A masterly effort by Capablanca.

16 *RUY LOPEZ*

MATCH / 1909

After a display of superior strategy Capablanca capably surmounts all the difficulties posed by a master tactician.

	White	*Black*
	CAPABLANCA	MARSHALL
1	P—K4	P—K4
2	N—KB3	N—QB3
3	B—N5	P—Q3
4	Castles	P—QR3
5	BxN ch	PxB
6	P—Q4	PxP

Here 6 . . . P—B3 gives Black a more solid defensive position.

7	NxP	B—Q2
8	R—K1	P—QB4
9	N—KB3	B—K2
10	N—B3	P—QB3

The immediate 10 . . . N—B3 can be answered effectively with 11 P—K5. Black's Queen-side Pawn complex is bound to be a source of trouble in any event.

11	B—B4	B—K3
12	Q—Q3	N—B3

13	QR—Q1!	P—Q4
14	N—KN5!	P—Q5

Practically forced, as 14 . . . PxP would leave Black with doubled, isolated Queen Bishop Pawns.

15	NxB	BPxN
16	N—R4!	. . . .

Now White threatens to win a Pawn with 17 Q—B4.

16	. . . .	Q—R4
17	P—QN3	R—Q1
18	N—N2!	N—R4

Black avoids 18 . . . QxP?? for then his Queen is trapped after 19 N—B4.

19	B—K5	Castles
20	N—B4	Q—N5
21	Q—R3!	. . . .

This wins a Pawn.

21	. . . .	P—N3
22	QxP ch	R—B2

DIAGRAM 16 Position after 22 . . . R—B2

Black (MARSHALL)

White (CAPABLANCA)

23	P—N4!	....

The winning move. If Black replies 23 . . . N—B3, White wins with 24 BxN, BxB; 25 N—Q6 etc.

Or if 23 . . . N—N2; 24 BxN, KxB; 25 N—K5 winning.

23	....	B—R5!?

An attempt to fish in troubled waters.

24	PxN	BxP ch
25	K—R1	....

Now Black realizes that 25 . . . BxR is refuted by 26 PxP, PxP; 27 QxP ch, K—B1; 28 N—Q6, R—B8 ch; 29 K—N2 etc.

25	....	Q—B6

Threatens 26 . . . Q—B6 mate.

26	R—K3!!	....

If now 26 . . . PxR?; 27 RxR mate. Or 26 . . . BxR; 27 PxP, PxP; 28 QxNP ch, K—B1; 29 N—Q6, R/Q1—Q2; 30 B—N7 ch! and wins.

26	....	QxBP
27	R/K3—Q3	Q—K7
28	N—Q6	RxN
29	BxR	B—K8

Again Black threatens mate. But White gets the jump on him.

30	Q—K8 ch	K—N2
31	P—R6 ch!	Resigns

For after 31 . . . KxP; 32 QxR White is a Rook ahead and has the mate covered. To outplay the great master of attack in this sparkling fashion was no mean achievement.

17 *QUEEN'S GAMBIT DECLINED*

NEW YORK STATE CHAMPIONSHIP / 1910

Black's listless handling of the opening allows Capablanca to obtain a powerful development which leads to an overwhelming attack.

	White	*Black*
	CAPABLANCA	JAFFE
1	P—Q4	P—Q4
2	N—KB3	N—KB3
3	P—K3	P—B3
4	P—B4	P—K3

Simpler is 4 . . . B—B4.

5	N—B3	QN—Q2
6	B—Q3	B—Q3
7	Castles	Castles
8	P—K4	Px K P
9	NxP	NxN
10	BxN	N—B3
11	B—B2	P—KR3

Black fears B—N5 followed by Q—Q3 threatening BxN and QxP mate. But this weakening of the King-side will prove intolerable.

12	P—QN3	P—QN3
13	B—N2	B—N2
14	Q—Q3	. . . .

Now there is a latent threat of P—Q5 followed by BxN and Q—R7 mate. This provokes a new weakness which quickly proves fatal to Black.

14	. . . .	P—N3
15	QR—K1	N—R4

He should have tried 15 . . . Q—K2 for reasons that will soon become clear.

16 B—B1! K—N2

DIAGRAM 17 Position after 16 . . . K—N2

Black (JAFFE)

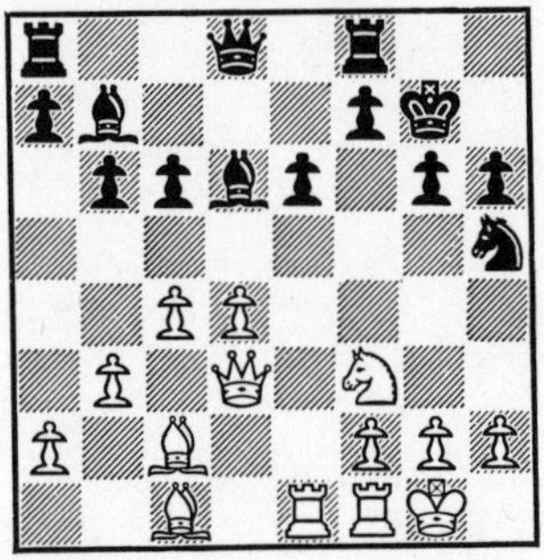

White (CAPABLANCA)

17 RxP! N—B3

If 17 . . . PxR; 18 QxP ch, K—R1; 19 Q—R7 mate.

18 N—K5! P—B4

Here 18 . . . BxN was necessary. The move actually played allows a quick finish, as does 18 . . . PxR; 19 QxP ch, K—R1; 20 QxP ch, K—N1; 21 Q—N6 ch, K—R1; 22 R—K1, Q—K1; 23 Q—R6 ch, K—N1; 24 R—K3 followed by R—N3 ch.

19 BxP ch! KxB
20 NxBP ch! Resigns

Just in time to stop mate. An elegant attack.

Sammy Reshevsky

BY WAY OF prefacing the collection of his best games, *Reshevsky on Chess*, Sammy Reshevsky ruefully described the lot of a child prodigy:

> To achieve world-wide fame at the age of eight is a mixed blessing. Such was my lot in life. I was a "chess prodigy" and my childhood, from the time I left my native Poland in 1920, consisted of a series of public exhibitions throughout Europe and the United States. Wherever I went, great crowds turned out to see me play. For four years, I was on public view. People stared at me, poked at me, tried to hug me, asked me questions. Professors measured my cranium and psychoanalyzed me. Reporters interviewed me and wrote fanciful stories about my future. Photographers were forever aiming their cameras at me.
>
> It was, of course, an unnatural life for a child, but it had its compensations and I cannot truthfully say that I did not enjoy it. There was the thrill of traveling from city to city with my family, the excitement of playing hundreds of games of chess and winning most of them, the knowledge that there was something "special" about the way I played chess, although I didn't know why.
>
> I was constantly being asked how I was able to play such strong chess as a child, but of course I did not know the answer. I could sing and I could ride a bicycle and I could play chess, but I didn't know how or why I could do these

things. I sang because I liked to sing—and I played chess because I liked to play chess. That was all I knew.

I had never studied the game. I was too young for that. I just picked it up from watching my father play at home. When I was four years old, I was able to play well enough to defeat most of the players in our village. By the time I was six, I had played with many Polish masters in Lodz and Warsaw, including Grandmaster Akiba Rubinstein, and had established a local reputation by giving simultaneous exhibitions in the leading cities of Poland.

In 1920, when I was eight years old, my career as a "chess prodigy" began in earnest. Accompanied by my parents, I toured the capitals of Europe, giving exhibitions at Berlin, Vienna, Paris, London and other cities. . . .

Then followed two years of incessant exhibitions in the United States, topped off by participation in a master tournament. The wonder of those years is perhaps not so much what Reshevsky achieved as the fact that he did not collapse under the physical strain.

Early in 1924 Reshevsky was withdrawn from circulation and given a chance to grow up as a normal child and to acquire a good education. With two minor exceptions he took no part in tournament play until 1931.

His reappearance in chess competition was by no means painless. He suffered from lack of practice and from unfamiliarity with opening theory. Though immediately recognized as a strong player, he produced games that were labored, long-winded, and rather uninspired. However, with his victory in the 1936 American championship tournament he established his rightful place in the front rank of masters, a position he has retained to the present day.

18 *RUY LOPEZ*

SIMULTANEOUS EXHIBITION / BERLIN / 1920

After coming out of the opening with a freer position, the boy wonder increases his positional advantage and winds up with a neat finesse.

	White	*Black*
	RESHEVSKY	ZABLUDOVSKY
1	P—K4	P—K4
2	N—KB3	N—QB3
3	B—N5	P—Q3

This defense generally leaves Black with a cramped position.

4	P—Q4	PxP
5	NxP	B—Q2
6	N—QB3	NxN
7	QxN	N—B3
8	Castles	P—KR3?
9	P—B4	BxB
10	NxB	P—R3
11	N—B3	B—K2
12	P—KR3	. . . .

To prepare for P—KN4 (after Black castles), and also with a view to playing Q—B2 followed by B—K3 without being disturbed by . . . N—N5.

12	. . . .	Castles
13	Q—B2	N—K1

Too timid.

14	P—KN4	P—QB3
15	B—K3	P—QB4?

Black's Pawn moves are unfortunate.

16	QR—Q1	P—QN3
17	P—K5	Q—B2
18	N—Q5	Q—N2
19	Q—N2	....

Threatening to win Black's Queen with N—B6 ch.

19	....	R—R2
20	KR—K1	PxP

White was threatening to win with 21 NxB ch, QxN; 22 PxP, NxP; 23 BxP etc.

21	PxP	B—R5
22	B—B2	BxB ch
23	QxB	K—R1?
24	P—K6!	P—B3
25	N—B4!	K—R2

DIAGRAM 18 Position after 25 . . . K—R2

Black (ZABLUDOVSKY)

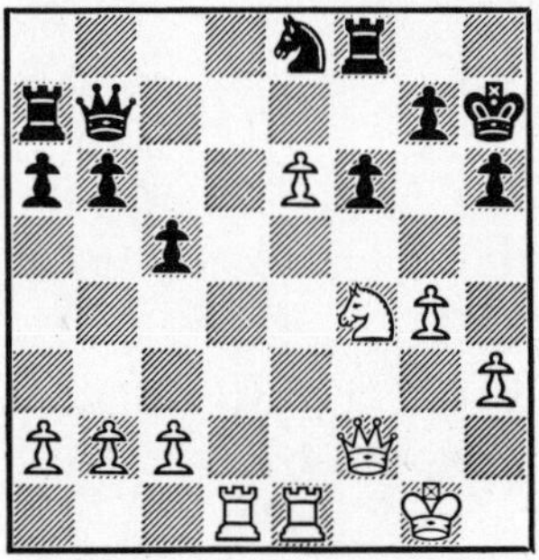

White (RESHEVSKY)

26	P—K7	....

Another way is 26 N—N6!, R—N1 (if 26 . . . KxN; 27 Q—B5 mate); 27 Q—B5 and Black is helpless against the threat of 28 N—B8 dbl ch, K—R1; 29 Q—R7 mate.

26	....	R—B2
27	R—Q8	R—R1
28	Q—N2!	QxQ ch

Black hopes for 29 KxQ?, RxP!

29	NxQ!	Resigns

For if 29 . . . RxP; 30 RxR, because the other White Rook is protected. White played with all the aplomb of a veteran.

19 *KING'S GAMBIT*

SIMULTANEOUS EXHIBITION / BERLIN / 1920

A real Morphy game, this one. White's snappy attacking play leads to an amusing finish.

	White	*Black*
	RESHEVSKY	DOERY
1	P—K4	P—K4
2	P—KB4	PxP
3	B—B4	B—K2
4	N—KB3	B—R5 ch

Inferior to the modern (developing) move 4 . . . N—KB3, which gives Black an excellent game.

5	P—KN3!?	....

More venturesome than 5 K—B1. Whether White will get value for his investment of several Pawns is a moot point.

5	....	PxP
6	Castles	PxP ch
7	K—R1	N—KR3?

Black has a safer alternative in 7 . . . B—B3. Then if 8 P—K5, P—Q4!; 9 PxB, NxP; 10 B—N3, N—K5 with good chances for Black (analyzed by Philidor in 1749!).

8	P—Q4	Q—K2

The book line 8 . . . P—Q4; 9 BxN, QPxB; 10 N—K5!, PxB; 11 NxP, Q—K2; 12 NxR, QxP ch; 13 KxP, B—N5; 14 N—B3! also gives White the better of it.

9	BxN	PxB
10	N—K5	B—B3
11	Q—R5	R—B1

Black seems to have countered the pressure on his King Bishop Pawn quite efficiently.

DIAGRAM 19 Position after 11 . . . R—B1

Black (DOERY)

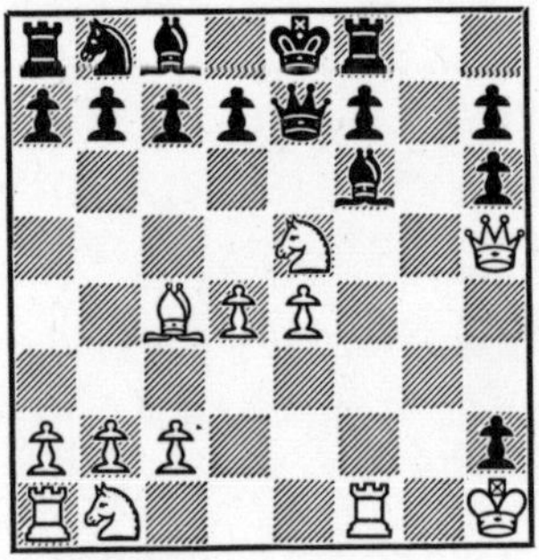

White (RESHEVSKY)

12	NxBP!	QxP ch

After 12 . . . RxN; 13 BxR ch, QxB; 14 QxQ ch, KxQ; 15 P—K5 and White wins without any trouble.

13	KxP	QxBP ch

Black must move his Queen as White is threatening N—Q6 dbl ch.

However, 13 . . . Q—N3 would not do in view of 14 R—K1 ch, B—K2; 15 RxB ch!, KxR; 16 Q—K5 ch and Black must give up his Queen.

14	K—N3	B—R5 ch

Black gives up the ghost, as he realizes that 14 . . . R—N1 ch fails because of 15 N—N5 dis ch, R—N3; 16 RxB, for example 16 . . . PxN; 17 B—B7 ch or 16 . . . QxB; 17 RxR etc.

15	QxB	QxB
16	Q—Q8 mate	

A sophisticated game by Sammy.

20 *BIRD'S OPENING*

SIMULTANEOUS EXHIBITION / HANNOVER / 1920

The wiles of an eight-year-old prove too much for Black in this game.

	White	*Black*
	RESHEVSKY	TRAUBE
1	P—KB4	P—K3
2	N—KB3	P—Q4
3	P—KN3	N—KB3
4	B—N2	B—Q3
5	P—Q4	N—B3

Rather cumbersome. Black can get a good game with 5 . . . P—B4 or 5 . . . QN—Q2.

6	N—K5	N—K2
7	B—K3	. . . .

Also rather clumsy. The logical move is 7 P—B4.

7	....	P—B3
8	P—QR3	P—KR3?
9	N—Q2	N—Q2
10	P—B4	P—QN3
11	P—QN4	P—B3?

DIAGRAM 20 Position after 11 . . . P—B3?

Black (TRAUBE)

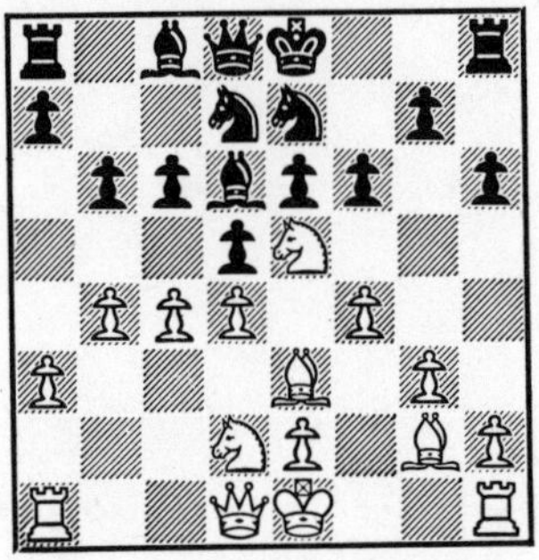

White (RESHEVSKY)

Now comes a clever sacrifice.

12	NxP!	NxN
13	PxP	PxP
14	BxP	B—N2
15	Q—B2!	....

Double attack: he threatens the Knight at QB6 and also threatens mate as well.

Comparatively best for Black was 15 . . . Q—B2; 16 QR—B1, QR—B1; 17 Q—N6 ch, K—Q1; 18 QxNP, R—K1; 19 B—B2 and White has a winning position.

15	....	QR—B1??
16	Q—N6 ch	K—B1
17	Q—B7 mate	

Black was outwitted.

21 *KING'S GAMBIT DECLINED*

WHITE PLAYS BLINDFOLD / NEW YORK / 1920

A significant encounter in which the child prodigy plays quite fearlessly against a recognized master. Jaffe takes liberties, but not for long.

	White	*Black*
	JAFFE	RESHEVSKY
1	P—K4	P—K4
2	P—KB4	B—B4
3	N—KB3	P—Q3
4	P—QN4?	....

This is suitable only in a game against a very weak player.

4	....	BxP
5	P—B3	B—QB4
6	P—Q4	PxQP
7	PxP	B—N3

White's imposing center is less formidable than it looks.

8	B—B4	N—KB3

Black does not fear 9 P—K5 because of 9 . . . P—Q4!

9	Q—Q3	Castles

Black is already threatening . . . NxP.

10	Castles	R—K1

Sammy does not fear 11 P—K5, which could be answered by 11 . . . P—Q4!; 12 B—N5, P—B3; 13 PxN, PxB; 14 PxP, Q—B3 with an excellent game for Black.

11	QN—Q2	P—N3!

A very deep move, as will be seen.

12	P—B5	....

On 12 P—K5 Black has an excellent reply in 12 . . . B—KB4, thanks to his last move.

DIAGRAM 21 Position after 12 P—B5

Black (RESHEVSKY)

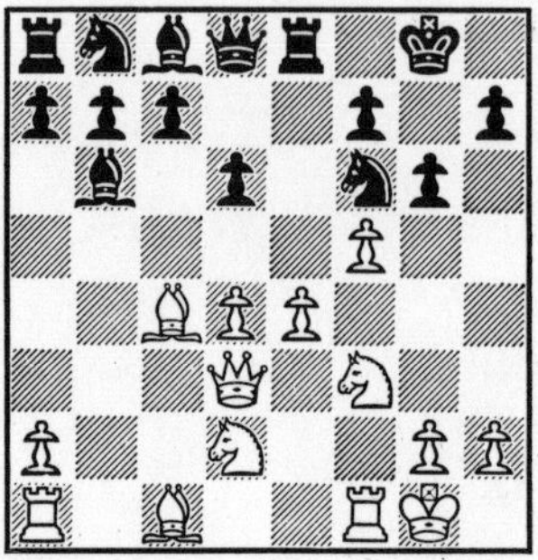

White (JAFFE)

12	....	P—Q4!

This forces White's Pawn center to cave in.

13	PxQP	BxBP
14	Q—N3	N—N5!
15	P—Q6	....

White still suffers from the delusion that he is the attacking party.

15	....	R—K6
16	BxP ch	K—N2

Now 17 Q—Q5?, P—B3 or 17 PxP?, QxBP costs White a piece.

17	Q—B4	B—Q6
	Resigns	

White has no compensation for the loss of the exchange. A sorry day for the master.

22 *KING'S GAMBIT*

SIMULTANEOUS EXHIBITION / ST. LOUIS / 1921

A sprightly attack is enlivened by a startling Queen sacrifice and an equally startling sequel.

	White	*Black*
	RESHEVSKY	BRUCKSTEIN
1	P—K4	P—K4
2	P—KB4	PxP
3	N—KB3	P—Q3?
4	P—Q4	B—N5
5	BxP	Q—B3?
6	B—N3	BxN?
7	PxB	P—QR3?
8	N—B3	N—B3
9	N—Q5!	....

Black's moves have no rhyme or reason, and White is steadily increasing his command of the board. Black's Queen must immediately return home, as 9 . . . QxP? loses the exchange at the very least.

9	....	Q—Q1
10	Q—Q2	KN—K2
11	B—QB4	P—QN4
12	B—N3	P—QR4?
13	P—QR4	P—N5
14	Q—Q3	Q—Q2
15	Castles/Q	R—B1

Black continues to flounder. As a result, he is unable to castle even at this late date.

16	Q—B4	....

Threatens 17 N—B6 ch! with a winning attack.

16	....	NxN
17	QxN/Q5	P—N3
18	P—K5!	N—Q1

Equally unattractive is 18 . . . PxP; 19 KR—K1, QxQ; 20 BxQ, N—K2; 21 BxKP, KR—N1; 22 B—KB6 etc.

19	KR—K1	N—K3
20	Q—K4	N—N4?

He should have tried 20 . . . B—R3 ch; 21 K—N1, Castles, although White would have a winning attack with 22 P—KB4 etc.

DIAGRAM 22 Position after 20 . . . N—N4?

Black (BRUCKSTEIN)

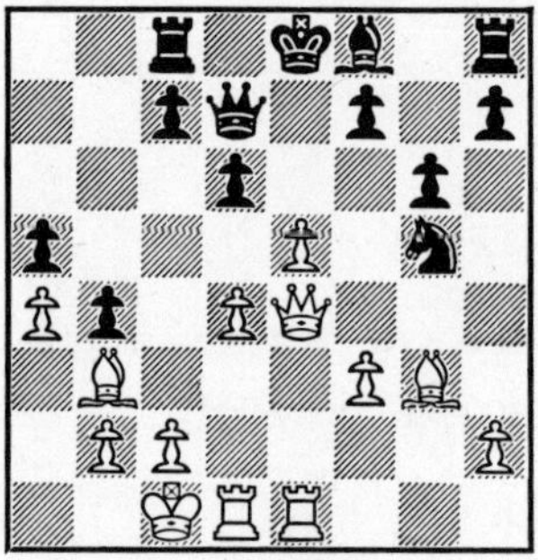

White (RESHEVSKY)

Black naturally expects White to move his attacked Queen.

21	PxP dis ch!	NxQ

Declining the Queen does no good: 21 . . . K—Q1; 22 Q—K5 and White wins.

22	RxN ch	Q—K3

A surprising reply, but 22 . . . K—Q1 would be ruinous in view of 23 B—R4 ch, B—K2; 24 RxB, QxP; 25 RxKBP ch, K—K1; 26 R—K1 ch.

23	RxQ ch!!	....

This move (instead of the obvious 23 BxQ) is the finest in the game, the idea being that after 23 . . . PxR; 24 BxP, R—R1; 25 PxP, B—R3 ch; 26 K—N1, K—K2; 27 B—R3 Black is helpless against P—Q5 followed by P—Q6 ch and P—Q7 etc.

23	....	K—Q2
24	R—B6	Resigns

Black has no compensation for the lost material. White's 21st and 23rd moves were very fine.

23 *QUEEN'S GAMBIT DECLINED*

NEW YORK / 1922

In this tournament young Sammy entered a contest with players of master strength for the first time. His victory over the famous international master, David Janowski, created a sensation. While the game is by no means perfect, it represents a phenomenal achievement for a ten-year-old child.

	White	*Black*
	JANOWSKI	RESHEVSKY
1	P—Q4	N—KB3
2	N—KB3	P—Q4
3	P—B4	P—K3
4	N—B3	QN—Q2
5	B—N5	B—K2
6	P—K3	P—B3
7	B—Q3	P—QR3
8	Castles	PxP
9	BxBP	N—N3?

This weak move—a consequence of Sammy's ignorance of the openings—leaves him with a permanently constricted game. The alternative 9 . . . P—QN4; 10 B—Q3, P—B4 followed by . . . B—N2 would have given him a much freer game.

10	B—Q3	KN—Q4
11	BxB	QxB
12	Q—Q2	. . . .

Here 12 N—K4—avoiding an exchange—is even more forceful.

12	. . . .	NxN
13	PxN	P—QB4
14	QR—N1	N—Q2
15	P—QR4	Castles
16	Q—B2	P—R3
17	KR—K1	P—QN3
18	R—N2	R—N1
19	KR—N1	. . . .

This pressure leaves Black in a very uncomfortable situation.

19	. . . .	Q—Q3
20	Q—K2!	P—QR4

A new and unavoidable weakness, for after 20 . . . R—R1 Black's position is too passive.

21	B—N5	R—Q1
22	P—R3	Q—B2
23	P—K4	N—B1
24	Q—K3	B—Q2
25	N—K5	. . . .

Janowski systematically strengthens his position in the center as a prelude to the coming King-side attack.

25	. . . .	B—K1
26	BxB	RxB
27	P—KB4	P—B3

28	N—B3	N—Q2
29	P—K5	P—B4

He closes the center, only to allow White to open a file on the King-side.

30	P—N4!	P—N3
31	NPxP	NPxP
32	P—Q5!	N—B1

On 32 . . . PxP White immediately regains the Pawn advantageously with 33 Q—Q3.

33	R—N2 ch	K—R2
34	P—B4	Q—B2
35	K—R2	N—N3
36	QR—N1	R—N1
37	P—Q6	Q—QN2

DIAGRAM 23 Position after 37 . . . Q—QN2

Black (RESHEVSKY)

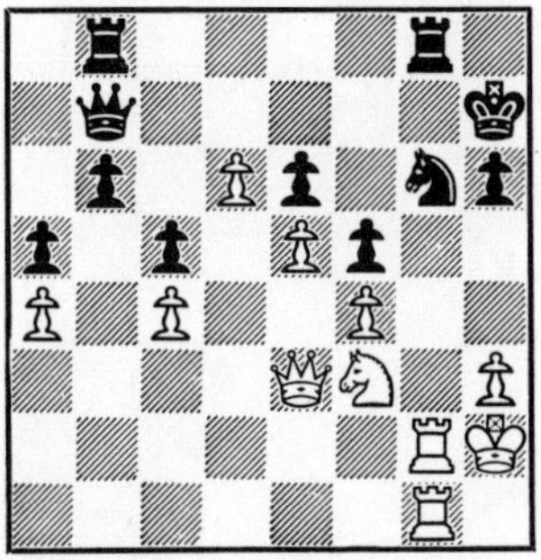

White (JANOWSKI)

White can now win with 38 N—N5 ch!, the main line being 38 . . . PxN; 39 RxP, R—N2; 40 Q—KN3!, Q—KB2; 41 R—R5 ch, K—N1; 42 R—R6, NxKP; 43 PxN!, RxQ; 44 RxR ch, Q—N2; 45 RxQ ch, KxR; 46 RxP and wins.

38	P—R4?	Q—B3
39	P—R5?	N—R1
40	N—N5 ch	....

At this point, however, Black has a viable defense.

40	....	PxN
41	PxP	N—N3!!

A resource which would do credit to a more experienced player. White's dangerous passed Pawns are stopped dead in their tracks—at least for a while.

42	R—N3	K—N2
43	R—R3	R—KR1
44	PxN	RxR ch
45	KxR	....

White would have been well advised to make the draw comparatively simple: 45 QxR!, R—KR1; 46 Q—R6 ch!, K—N1! (not 46 . . . RxQ ch; 47 PxR ch and White forces the queening of a Pawn, for example 47 . . . K—N1; 48 P—N7!, Q—K1; 49 P—R7 ch!, KxP; 50 P—N8/Q ch!, QxQ; 51 RxQ, KxR; 52 P—Q7 etc.); 47 P—N7!, R—R2; 48 K—N3, RxQ; 49 PxR, Q—K5; 50 P—Q7 and Black must take a draw by perpetual check.

45	....	R—R1 ch
46	K—N3	QxRP
47	Q—KB3	P—B5 ch
48	K—N4	Q—B7
49	QxP	Q—K7 ch
50	K—N3	Q—Q6 ch
51	K—N2	Q—K7 ch
52	K—N3	Q—R7 ch
53	K—B3	R—KB1
54	Q—B6 ch!	....

Now White is willing to draw. He anticipates 54 . . . RxQ ch; 55 NPxR ch, K—N1; 56 P—Q7, Q—Q7; 57 P—N7! and the standing threat of P—B7 ch forces Black to take a perpetual check.

54	....	K—N1!
55	P—Q7	RxQ ch

DIAGRAM 24 Position after 55 . . . RxQ ch

Black (RESHEVSKY)

White (JANOWSKI)

Now White has a last chance to draw with 56 KPxR!, Q—Q7; 57 P—B7 ch, K—N2; 58 R—KR1! and now Black must take a perpetual check, for if 58 . . . QxQP?; 59 R—R7 ch, KxP; 60 P—B8/N ch and White wins.

56	NPxR?	Q—Q7
57	R—KR1	Q—Q6 ch!

Very fine: 57 . . . QxQP? loses after 58 P—B7 ch, K—N2; 59 R—R7 ch etc.

58	K—N2	....

If the King goes to B4 or B2, Black replies 58 . . . Q—B4 ch! Then if White's King goes to the Knight file, 59 . . . QxNP ch wins for Black. On the other hand, if White plays the King to the King file, Black wins easily with 59 . . . QxKP ch followed by 60 . . . QxP.

58	....	QxNP ch

Now Black has a certain win, as he will be able to pick up the Queen Pawn as well.

59	K—B2	Q—B4 ch
60	K—N2	Q—N5 ch
61	K—R2	Q—K7 ch
62	K—R3	Q—Q6 ch
63	K—R4	QxP
64	R—KN1 ch	K—B1
65	K—N5	Q—Q5
	Resigns	

An impressive victory for Sammy. This is a game that would have taxed a much older and more experienced player.

24 *QUEEN'S GAMBIT DECLINED*

WESTERN CHAMPIONSHIP / 1927

Reshevsky neatly refutes his opponent's inexact opening play.

	White	*Black*
	RESHEVSKY	PALMER
1	P—Q4	P—K3
2	N—KB3	P—Q4
3	P—B4	P—QB3
4	P—K3	N—B3
5	N—B3	QN—Q2
6	Q—B2	B—Q3
7	B—Q3	PxP
8	BxBP	P—QN4

Though playable this move will lead to some difficulties. Simple and good would be 8 . . . P—K4.

9	B—Q3	P—QR3
10	B—Q2	P—B4
11	P—QR4!	....

Disarranging Black's Queen-side Pawns in the event that he chooses his best course: 11 . . . P—N5; 12 N—K4, NxN; 13 BxN, R—R2.

11	....	BPxP?

A mistake that brings White's King Knight into very strong play.

12	KNxP	P—N5
13	N—K4	N—K4?

Incredible as it seems, this plausible move loses a piece. However, if 13 . . . B—K2; 14 N—B6 wins: 14 . . . Q—B2; 15 NxB, QxQ; 16 BxQ, KxN; 17 BxP ch, K—Q1; 18 N—Q6 etc.

DIAGRAM 25 Position after 13 . . . N—K4?

Black (PALMER)

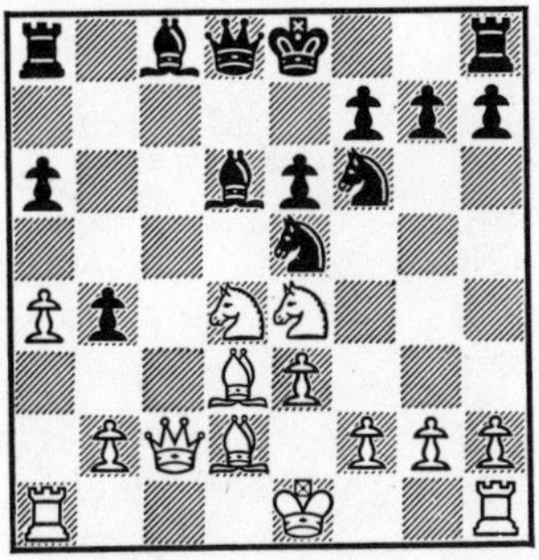

White (RESHEVSKY)

14	N—B6!	....

This wins a piece, for if 14 . . . N/K4xN; 15 QxN ch etc. Or 14 . . . NxB ch; 15 QxN with the same result.

14	....	Q—B2
15	NxB ch	QxN
16	NxN	B—N2

Now Black belatedly realizes that 16 . . . QxN is answered by 17 Q—B6 ch with devastating effect.

17	N—B4	Q—Q4
18	P—K4	Q—Q5
19	B—K3	Resigns

Further play is hopeless. Sammy has neatly refuted his opponent's unsound play.

25 *GRUENFELD DEFENSE (IN EFFECT)*

WESTERN CHAMPIONSHIP / 1933

This final game of Reshevsky's gives a hint of his mature style. We see here what subtle means he employs to gain the advantage in a seemingly colorless position.

	White	*Black*
	RESHEVSKY	MICHELSEN
1	P—Q4	P—Q4
2	P—QB4	P—QB3
3	N—KB3	P—KN3
4	N—B3	B—N2
5	P—K3	N—B3
6	Q—N3	Castles
7	B—Q3	PxP

Black is better off maintaining the center with 7 . . . P—K3. He now begins what appears to be a freeing action, but in actuality he only opens up lines for White's pieces.

8	BxBP	QN—Q2
9	N—KN5	P—K3

10	Castles	N—N3
11	B—K2	KN—Q2
12	N—B3	P—K4

On the face of it Black has achieved a very satisfactory position. It is just at this point that Reshevsky displays his strategic mastery.

13	R—Q1	Q—K2
14	P—K4!	PxP
15	NxP	N—B4
16	Q—B2	N—K3
17	N—B3!	....

It is essential to avoid exchanges if the constriction policy is to succeed.

17	....	B—Q2

This Bishop has no real prospects of satisfactory development.

18	P—QR4!	QR—Q1
19	B—K3	KR—K1
20	P—R5!	N—QB1

Black's pieces are badly huddled together.

21	P—K5!	....

Very strong, the immediate positional threat being N—K4—Q6. In his anxiety to avoid this, Black stumbles into something worse.

21	....	P—B3
22	PxP	BxP
23	N—K4	B—N2

To allow the exchange of this valuable Bishop would be a positional disaster, but now his position crumbles anyway.

DIAGRAM 26 Position after 23 . . . B—N2

Black (MICHELSEN)

White (RESHEVSKY)

24	Q—N3!	. . . .

White threatens to win the exchange with B—KN5, and he also threatens QxP followed by BxP with an easy win.

24	. . . .	P—N3
25	B—KN5	Q—B2
26	BxR	RxB

Or 26 . . . NxB; 27 B—B4!, B—K3; 28 RxN!, BxB; 29 RxR ch and wins.

27	B—B4!	Resigns

For he is helpless against the double threat of 28 RxB or 28 N—N5. A first-class example of positional play.

Bobby Fischer

THOUGH HE IS the most recent of the child prodigies, Bobby Fischer bids fair to outdistance his illustrious forerunners.

He was born in Chicago on March 9, 1943, and learned the moves at the age of six from his sister Joan, who was then eleven. His aptitude for the game was immediately noticeable, and he soon began to haunt chess clubs. By 1956 he was fully launched as a tournament player, winning the United States Junior Championship that year and tying for fourth in the United States Open Tournament.

On the strength of these achievements the youngster was invited to play in the Rosenwald Tournament with an imposing entry headed by Reshevsky and Bisguier. Despite his lack of experience in master play, Bobby turned in a very creditable score, tying for eighth place with 4½—6½ (two wins, four losses, five draws).

But the feature of his performance that created a sensation was his remarkable victory against Donald Byrne, which the authoritative observer Hans Kmoch immediately dubbed "the game of the century." Kmoch, who has known all the greats and near-greats on the international chess scene for almost five decades, is not easily carried away by enthusiasm. But this time he fairly rhapsodized in *Chess Review*:

The following game, a stunning masterpiece of combination play performed by a boy of thirteen against a formidable opponent, matches the finest on record in the history of chess prodigies.

It was now clear that the United States had acquired a chess star of the first magnitude. But even his staunchest admirers could hardly have expected that only a year later, at the age of fourteen, Bobby would win the United States Championship against an even stronger field, including the incumbent champion, Sammy Reshevsky. The former child prodigy had been dethroned by the current child prodigy.

Just to prove that this amazing feat was no accident, Bobby thereafter won the title in every championship tournament in which he participated—a total of seven times to date. On the international scene he also acquitted himself creditably, quickly establishing a reputation as one of the world's great masters.

His most notable feat in international chess to date has been his impressive first prize in the Stockholm Interzonal Tournament of 1962, where he was matched against a choice field of some of the world's outstanding players.

At nineteen Bobby had achievements to his credit which outranked those of any other player in the history of chess at a comparable age. But what is perhaps even more remarkable is the rounded and mature quality of his style. In the openings he is studiously attuned to all the latest innovations and finesses—a marked point of difference from Capablanca and Reshevsky. In the middle game he is equally at home in refined positional play and daring attacking play. If any part of the game can be said to be his special domain, however, it is the end game, for which he has the patience, the tenacity, and the delicacy of judgment that distinguish the elect of the chess world.

Among all the components of Bobby's reputation there is no element of modesty. He has been quoted as saying, for example, "I know that I deserve to be World Champion and I know I can beat Botvinnik. There's no one alive I can't beat."

In the light of what Bobby has accomplished so far in so

little time, such a remark cannot be dismissed as empty boastfulness. In fact, his observation might reasonably be put down as an example of serene self-confidence, justifiable, proper, and even endearing in a mettlesome youth. But time will tell.

26 *RETI OPENING (IN EFFECT)*

UNITED STATES OPEN CHAMPIONSHIP / 1956

In the twenties Richard Reti astounded the chess world with his novel technique of attacking center Pawns from the wings. Here the youthful player of the White pieces adopts the same method with a matter-of-fact approach that seems uncanny.

	White	*Black*
	FISCHER	LAPIKEN
1	N—KB3	N—KB3
2	P—KN3	P—Q4
3	B—N2	B—B4
4	Castles	P—K3
5	P—Q3	P—B3
6	QN—Q2	N—R3
7	P—QR3	N—B4
8	P—B4	....

The key move of Reti's system. The pressure on Black's center is strengthened by this flank thrust.

8	....	P—QN4?

A massive positional blunder. By undermining his Queen Bishop Pawn, Black undermines his hold on the long diagonal.

9	N—Q4!	....

Excellent. He gains time by attacking the weakened Queen Bishop Pawn. Meanwhile his hitherto passive King Bishop suddenly takes on a menacing role.

9	....	Q—Q2
10	NxB	PxN

The exchange has further weakened Black's position.

11	N—N3!	....

Now White threatens 12 B—N5, with the further threat of inflicting a tripled isolated King Bishop Pawn on Black and at the same time undermining the support of his Queen Pawn still further through the removal of Black's protective Knight.

Black has nothing to hope for from 11 . . . QPxP; 12 PxP, PxP; 13 N—R5, with a winning positional advantage for White.

11	....	P—KR3
12	B—K3	N—K3

The alternative 12 . . . NxN; 13 QxN, P—Q5 is refuted by 14 PxP! etc. This is a good example of White's power along the long diagonal.

13	N—Q4	P—N3

The alternative 13 . . . NxN; 14 BxN, B—K2; 15 PxNP, PxP; 16 Q—N3 (threatening to win a Pawn), R—Q1; 17 QR—B1 leaves White with all the play.

14	Q—N3!	....

Very strong. As Black cannot go in for 14 . . . QPxP; 15 PxP, NxN; 16 BxN, QxB; 17 BxP ch followed by 18 BxR, he must give his Queen Knight Pawn additional protection. But this gives Fischer the opportunity for a neat combination.

14	....	QR—N1

DIAGRAM 27 Position after 14 . . . QR—N1

Black (LAPIKEN)

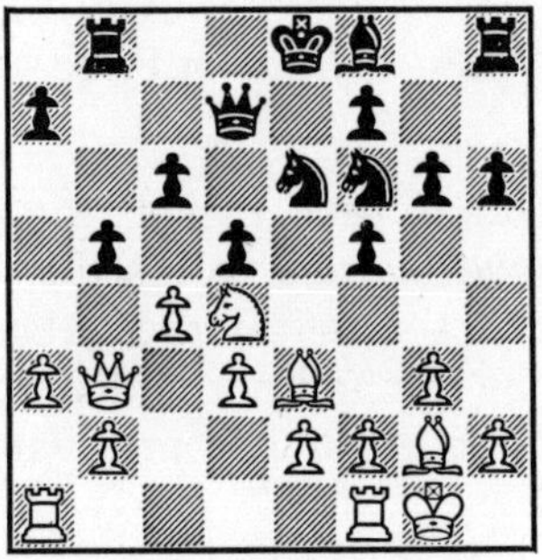

White (FISCHER)

15	NxQBP!	. . . .

What makes this sacrifice particularly delectable is that it validates the basic theme: pressure on the long diagonal.

15	. . . .	QxN
16	PxQP	N—B4

Black wriggles.

17	Q—B3!	Q—Q3

A neat variation is 17 . . . Q—N3; 18 P—QN4, N—R5; 19 Q—K5 ch winning Black's Queen.

18	BxN	QxB
19	QxN	Resigns

An amusing finish. If Black moves his attacked Rook, White wins the other one with 20 Q—K5 ch.

27 *GRUENFELD DEFENSE (IN EFFECT)*

ROSENWALD TOURNAMENT / NEW YORK / 1956

First Brilliancy Prize

This masterpiece has been called "the game of the century." While we have learned to distrust superlatives, this is one game that deserves all the praise that has been lavished on it. It has the additional distinction of being the most dazzling and the most profound game ever won by a child prodigy.

	White	*Black*
	D. BYRNE	FISCHER
1	N—KB3	N—KB3
2	P—B4	P—KN3
3	N—B3	B—N2
4	P—Q4	Castles
5	B—B4	P—Q4

A promising Pawn sacrifice which White prefers not to accept, for after 6 PxP, NxP; 7 NxN, QxN; 8 BxP, N—R3; 9 B—N3, B—B4 (threatening . . . N—N5); 10 P—QR3, QR—B1 and Black has strong pressure for his Pawn.

6	Q—N3	....

DIAGRAM 28 Position after 6 Q—N3

Black (FISCHER)

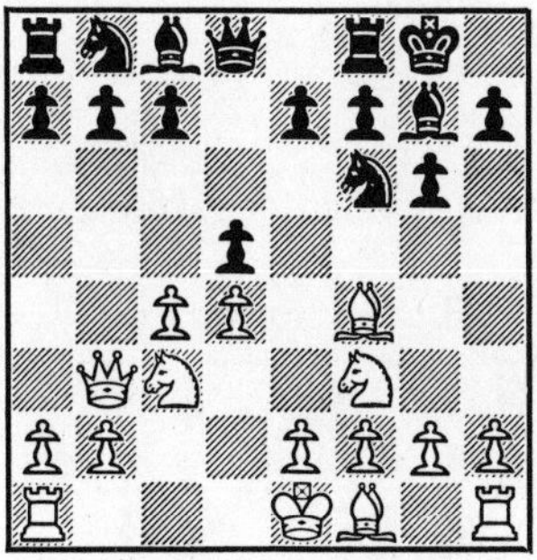

White (BYRNE)

White's early Queen move "puts the question" to Black's Queen Pawn. Black must now arrive at a decision about his coming policy in the center.

6	....	PxP
7	QxBP	P—B3
8	P—K4	QN—Q2

White has a magnificent Pawn center, forcing Black to seek compensation by active deployment of his pieces.

9	R—Q1	N—N3
10	Q—B5?	....

Some danger is always attached to early Queen moves, and this one only compounds the danger: White's Queen is going too far afield. Instead, White had a safer line in 10 Q—N3 or 10 Q—Q3.

10	....	B—N5

Now Black has in mind some such continuation as 11 . . . KN—Q2; 12 Q—R3, P—K4; 13 PxP, Q—K1 and Black recovers his Pawn with a good game.

11	B—KN5?	....

Very plausible: the idea is that 11 . . . KN—Q2? would lose Black's King Pawn.

However, if White had had any inkling of Black's fantastic resources, he would have quietly continued his development with 11 B—K2.

DIAGRAM 29 Position after 11 B—KN5?

Black (FISCHER)

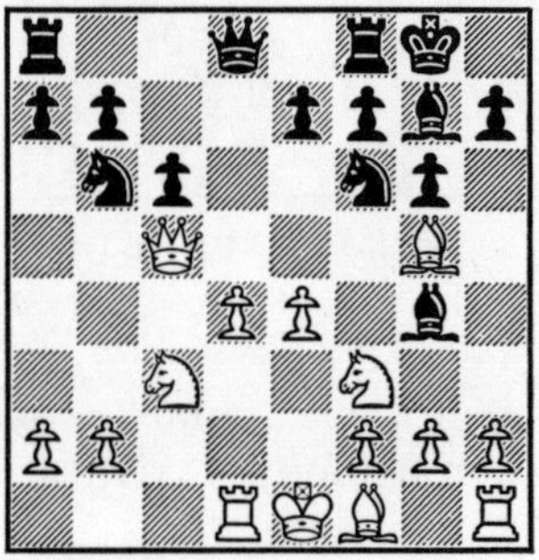

White (BYRNE)

11 . . . . N—R5!!!

One of the most magnificent moves ever made on the chessboard. From the practical point of view it has the additional psychological advantage of looking like the crassest kind of blunder.

The reply 12 NxN is self-evident, as White can answer 12 . . . NxP with 13 QxKP. But then comes the murderous reply 13 . . . Q—R4 ch and White is lost: 14 N—B3, NxN threatening . . . R—K1. Or 14 P—N4, QxN and again the threat of . . . R—K1 is decisive. Should White attempt 15 QxN, KR—K1; 16 N—K5, he gets hit with 16 . . . QxR mate. Or 15 QxN, KR—K1; 16 B—K7, BxN and Black wins after 17 PxB, B—B3 or 17 QxB, RxB ch; 18 B—K2, QR—K1; 19 R—Q2, QxNP etc.

But this by no means exhausts the fascinating possibilities after 12 NxN, NxP. Consider 13 BxP, NxQ; 14

BxQ, NxN; 15 B—KN5, BxN; 16 PxB, NxP and Black must win the ending: he is a Pawn to the good and all the remaining White Pawns are isolated.

Finally there is this possibility: 12 NxN, NxP; 13 Q—N4, NxB; 14 NxN, BxR; 15 KxB, BxP. In this case Black has a Rook and two Pawns for two Knights—a fair material equivalent. But White's King is in danger and his pieces are scattered.

12	Q—R3	NxN
13	PxN	NxP!!

Another surprise attacking move which White had thought he was preventing.

14	BxP	Q—N3!

Black's skill in finding new resources must be very frustrating for his opponent. After 15 BxR, BxB; 16 Q—N3 there follows 16 . . . NxQBP! Then on 17 QxN? Black has 17 . . . B—N5 winning the White Queen. Or if 17 QxQ, PxQ and Black picks up a second Pawn for the exchange, remaining with a winning game. Finally, on 17 R—Q2 Black has 17 . . . R—K1 ch with a lasting attack.

15	B—B4	NxQBP!

Another beautiful move. The immediate point is 16 QxN, KR—K1 and Black recovers the piece with a Pawn to the good.

16	B—B5	. . . .

Still keeping Black's Knight under attack, White attacks the Queen. Seemingly Black must lose some material.

16	. . . .	KR—K1 ch
17	K—B1	. . . .

DIAGRAM 30 Position after 17 K—B1

Black (FISCHER)

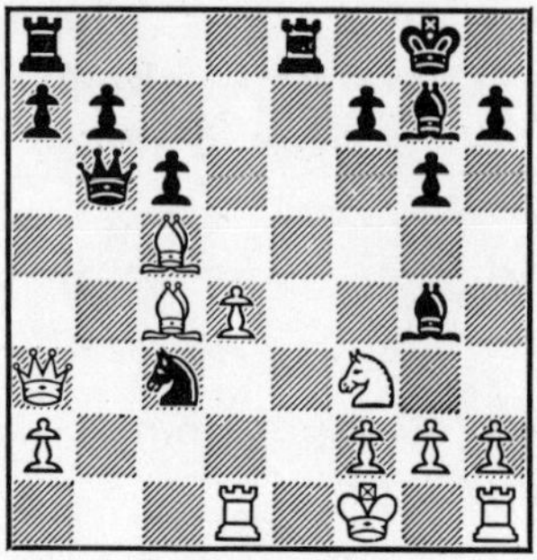

White (BYRNE)

Black's only hope of saving himself is apparently 17 . . . N—N4. But then comes 18 BxP ch! and Black is lost: 18 . . . KxB; 19 Q—N3 ch, B—K3; 20 N—N5 ch etc.—or 18 . . . K—R1; 19 BxQ, NxQ; 20 BxR etc.

17	....	B—K3!!

A stunning resource. Black's ingenuity seems inexhaustible.

White selects the most obvious reply, which loses. However, there is no good move. For example, 18 BxB?, Q—N4 ch and Black forces mate: 19 K—N1, N—K7 ch; 20 K—B1, N—N6 dbl ch; 21 K—N1, Q—B8 ch!; 22 RxQ, N—K7 mate.

A charming alternative possibility is 18 QxN, QxB!; 19 PxQ, BxQ and Black's Pawn ahead assures him an endgame win.

Finally, if 18 B—Q3 Black extricates himself with 18 . . . N—N4!; 19 Q—N4, Q—B2; 20 P—QR4, P—QR4!

18	BxQ	BxB ch
19	K—N1	N—K7 ch
20	K—B1	NxP dis ch!

Now the Knight will be protected on QB6 two moves later, enabling Black to achieve a substantial plus in material.

21	K—N1	N—K7 ch
22	K—B1	N—B6 dis ch
23	K—N1	PxB

Attacking White's Queen and still keeping his Rook under attack. The reply 24 Q—B1? is out of the question because of 24 . . . N—K7 ch.

24	Q—N4	. . . .

Wistfully hoping for 24 . . . NxR; 25 QxB.

24	. . . .	R—R5!
25	QxP	NxR

With two Bishops and a Rook for the White Queen, Black has triumphantly concluded his splendid combination.

26	P—KR3	RxP
27	K—R2	NxP
28	R—K1	RxR
29	Q—Q8 ch	B—B1
30	NxR	B—Q4

Black can win easily enough by advancing his Queen-side Pawns; but the possibility of a mating attack is even more attractive.

31	N—B3	N—K5
32	Q—N8	P—QN4
33	P—R4	P—R4
34	N—K5	K—N2

Black frees his King Bishop for action.

35	K—N1	B—B4 ch
36	K—B1	. . . .

Now Black has a quick mate, but after 36 K—R2, B—Q3; 37 Q—K8, N—B3 is murderous.

36	....	N—N6 ch

Another way is 36 . . . R—KB7 ch; 37 K—K1 (if 37 K—N1, R—B5 dis ch followed by 38 . . . RxP mate), B—N5 ch; 38 K—Q1, B—N6 ch; 39 K—B1, R—B8 mate.

37	K—K1	....

Now the quickest mate is 37 . . . R—K7 ch; 38 K—Q1, B—N6 ch; 39 K—B1, B—R6 ch; 40 K—N1, R—K8 mate. But Fischer may have been pressed for time.

37	....	B—N5 ch
38	K—Q1	B—N6 ch
39	K—B1	N—K7 ch
40	K—N1	N—B6 ch
41	K—B1	R—QB7 mate

A fitting conclusion to a sensational game.

28 *RUY LOPEZ*

EASTERN STATES OPEN TOURNAMENT / 1956

In this fine game the fourteen-year-old victor displays two remarkable attributes of chess skill. One of these is obvious, the other not so obvious. The brilliant and decisive 40 B—B7!! lends a touch of charm to the strong and forcible finish. But to the expert the feature of this game that is even more impressive is the mature, carefully thought-out position play that leads up to this fine finish.

	White	*Black*
	FISCHER	Di CAMILLO
1	P—K4	P—K4
2	N—KB3	N—QB3
3	B—N5	P—QR3
4	B—R4	N—B3

5	Castles	P—QN4
6	B—N3	P—Q3

Black's deviation from the regular order of moves allows White to play for the win of a Pawn with 7N—N5, P—Q4; 8 PxP, N—Q5!; 9 P—Q6, NxB; 10 PxP, QxP; 11 RPxN, P—KR3 and Black has a fine initiative for the Pawn.

7	P—B3	B—N5
8	P—KR3	....

A debatable move which weakens his castled position. The point is that later on Black can strive for . . . P—N4—5 in the hope of opening a file on the King-side in order to menace White's castled King. But somehow neither player seems to reckon with this possibility.

8	....	B—R4
9	P—Q3	B—K2
10	QN—Q2	....

DIAGRAM 31 Position after 10 QN—Q2

Black (DI CAMILLO)

White (FISCHER)

In line with the previous comment, Black can now get a strong game with 10 . . . Q—Q2!, intending . . . P—N4 followed by . . . P—KN5.

Nor can White very well play 11 P—N4?, for then comes 11 . . . NxNP; 12 PxN, QxP ch; 13 K moves, B—N4! with a winning attack (. . . B—B5 etc.).

10	....	Castles

After this colorless move the possibility of . . . P—N4 and . . . P—KN5 is ruled out, as Black's King-side would be shattered by such an advance. Understandably, the initiative soon passes to White.

11	R—K1	Q—Q2
12	N—B1	....

White is preparing to rid himself of the obnoxious pin.

12	....	N—R4
13	B—B2	P—R3
14	P—KN4!	....

The point of this clever move is that after 14 . . . NxNP; 15 PxN, QxP ch; 16 N—N3, QxN; White remains a piece ahead with 17 NxB.

14	....	B—N3

The Bishop has been deprived of any further usefulness.

15	N—N3	N—R2
16	N—B5	....

Always a powerful post for this Knight. Unfortunately for Black, he cannot very well play 16 . . . BxN as 17 NPxB would give White a powerful attack along the King Knight file.

16	....	N—N2

Casting about desperately for counterplay, Black tries to bring this Knight to K3. But White very cleverly nips this idea in the bud.

17	P—Q4!	....

Very well timed.

DIAGRAM 32 Position after 17 P—Q4!

Black (DI CAMILLO)

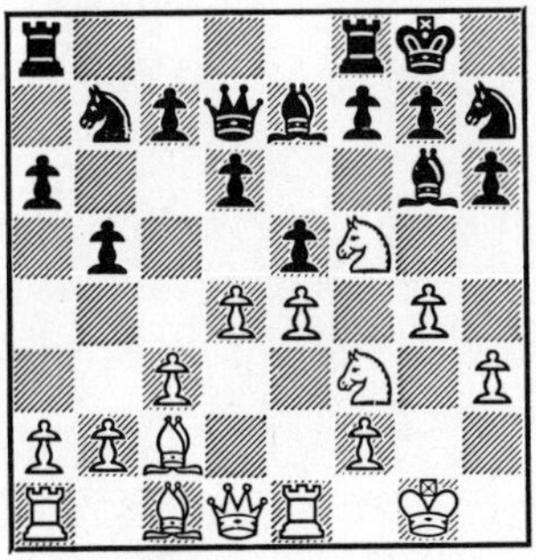

White (FISCHER)

Black cannot hold the center: for example, 17 . . . P—KB3?; 18 PxP, BxN; 19 NPxB, BPxP; 20 Q—Q5 ch winning a piece.

Or 17 . . . B—B3; 18 PxP and White still wins material.

17	. . . .	PxP
18	PxP	N—Q1

Now White can prevent . . . N—K3 with 19 P—Q5, but then 19 . . . B—B3 gives Black a game of sorts in view of the King Bishop fine diagonal. So:

19	NxB ch	QxN
20	P—Q5!	P—QB4
21	B—B4!	N—N2
22	B—KN3	KR—K1
23	P—QR4!	. . . .

Before proceeding to the positionally decisive P—K5, White first shakes up Black's Queen-side Pawns.

23	. . . .	Q—B3
24	PxP	PxP
25	K—N2	. . . .

White cold-bloodedly permits 25 . . . QxP, which can be answered advantageously with 26 R—QN1 and 27 RxP.

25	. . . .	N—N4
26	NxN	PxN
27	RxR	RxR
28	P—K5!	. . . .

In the strategical sense this is the winning move. White forces a passed Queen Pawn and undermines Black's Queen-side Pawns.

28	. . . .	BxB
29	QxB	PxP
30	BxP	Q—Q1
31	P—Q6!	. . . .

The power of the passed Pawn immediately makes itself felt. Black cannot play 31 . . . NxP because of 32 QxP and White wins the Queen Knight Pawn.

31	. . . .	P—B5
32	Q—K4	N—B4

And not 32 . . . NxP?; 33 BxN because White wins a piece.

33	Q—B6	N—Q6
34	R—K3	R—B1

Or 34 . . . NxB; 35 RxN, R—B1; 36 Q—Q5 and the threat of P—Q7 is decisive (if 36 . . . Q—Q2; 37 R—K7, Q—B3; 38 QxQ, RxQ; 39 R—K8 ch, K—R2; 40 P—Q7 and wins).

35	Q—N7	. . . .

And not 35 QxNP?, R—B4 because Black wins a piece.

35	. . . .	R—N1
36	Q—Q5	N—N5
37	Q—B5	N—Q6
38	Q—Q4	. . . .

White's powerful passed Pawn is the key to the play hereabouts. If now 38 . . . NxB; 39 RxN, R—N2; 40 Q—K4!, R—N1 forced; 41 Q—Q5 and White wins quickly.

38	....	R—N3
39	P—Q7!	R—N2

Apparently Black is about to dispose of the dangerous Pawn.

DIAGRAM 33 Position after 39 . . . R—N2

Black (DI CAMILLO)

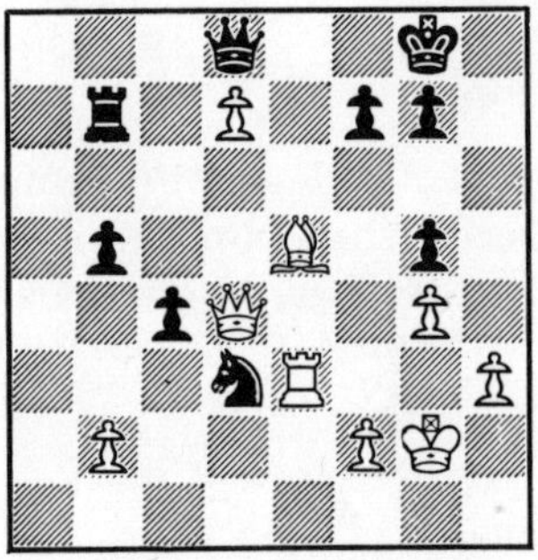

White (FISCHER)

40	B—B7!!	....

Very beautiful. Black is helpless against the double threat of BxQ or R—K8 ch.

40	....	N—B5 ch

A last hope. On 41 QxN? he saves himself with 41 . . . QxP, while 41 BxN? allows 41 . . . RxP.

41	K—B1	Resigns

Masterly play by White.

29 *SICILIAN DEFENSE*

MATCH / 1957

A fascinating game, imperfections and all. The best moves were never played.

	White	*Black*
	FISCHER	CARDOSO
1	P—K4	P—QB4
2	N—KB3	P—Q3
3	P—Q4	PxP
4	NxP	N—KB3
5	N—QB3	P—QR3
6	B—QB4	....

Fischer's trademark. It leads to complicated play, for example if 6 . . . NxP White can simply reply 7 NxN, P—Q4; 8 B—Q3, PxN; 9 BxKP with a fine lead in development, or he can try 7 BxP ch!, KxB; 8 Q—R5 ch winning back the piece advantageously.

6	....	P—K3
7	Castles!?	

DIAGRAM 34 Position after 7 Castles!?

Black (CARDOSO)

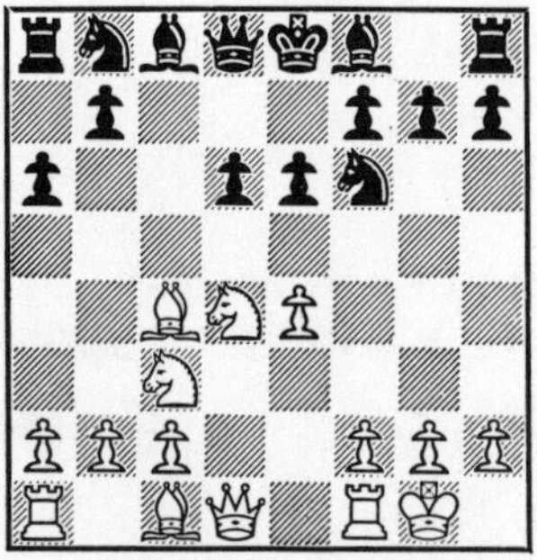

White (FISCHER)

7	....	B—K2

Black avoids the possibility of winning a Pawn by 7 . . . P—QN4; 8 B—N3 (the intended move), P—N5; 9 N—N1, NxP although he seems reasonably safe after 10 Q—B3, P—Q4.

Still another way to meet 10 Q—B3 in this line is 10 . . . B—N2 and if 11 B—R4 ch, N—Q2; 12 N—B6, Q—N3 (also good is 12 . . . KN—B4!); 13 QxN, R—B1! regaining the piece satisfactorily (but not 13 . . . P—Q4?; 14 Q—Q4! and White wins).

8	B—K3!	. . . .

A tricky move, the idea being that on 8 . . . P—QN4; 9 B—N3, P—N5?; 10 N—R4!, NxP? White wins with the remarkable move 11 N—KB5! In that event 11 . . . PxN will not do because of 12 Q—Q5 winning; while 11 . . . Castles is disastrous because of 12 NxB ch, QxN; 13 N—N6 and Black is lost.

8	. . . .	Castles
9	B—N3	N—B3
10	P—B4	. . . .

White starts a vigorous King-side attack.

10	. . . .	N—QR4
11	Q—B3	Q—B2
12	P—KN4	NxB

This allows White's attack to roll on almost unopposed. There is more counterattacking punch in 12 . . . N—B5 etc.

13	RPxN	R—N1

This tame move is a necessary prelude to . . . P—QN4, for if Black advances his Queen Knight Pawn at once, White can simply capture it.

14	P—N5	N—Q2
15	P—B5	N—K4
16	Q—N3	K—R1
17	N—B3!	. . . .

A good move which removes a vital Black defensive piece and at the same time prepares the entry of White's Rooks into the attack.

17	....	NxN ch
18	RxN	P—N4
19	Q—R4!	....

White threatens to demolish Black's position with 20 R—R3, P—R3; 21 P—B6 etc. The advanced Pawns have become irresistible.

19	....	PxP
20	PxP	Q--B3!

Counterplay on the long diagonal is Black's only chance. Right now he doesn't fear 21 R—R3? as 21 . . . BxBP will protect him against the mating threat.

21	QR—KB1	B—N2!

This immobilizes White's Rook at KB3. Still, accurate attacking play should win quickly for White.

22	B—Q4!?	....

Good enough to win, though later analysis indicated that 22 Q—R5! (threatening P—N6!) would win for White in a more straightforward fashion.

22	....	P—N5

The critical position has been reached.

DIAGRAM 35 Position after 22 . . . P—N5

Black (CARDOSO)

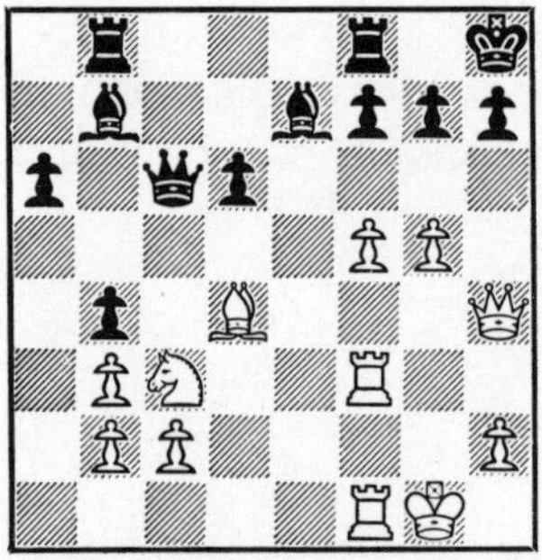

White (FISCHER)

Now 23 Q—R5! wins in all variations.

For example, if 23 . . . PxN; 24 P—N6!, KBPxP; 25 PxP, P—R3; 26 QxRP ch and mate next move.

Or 23 . . . K—N1; 24 P—B6, B—Q1; 25 PxP and Black can resign.

Finally, if 23 . . . P—B3; 24 P—N6, P—R3; 25 B—K3!, K—N1; 26 BxP and Black is helpless against the murderous threat of 27 BxP.

23	BxP ch?!	. . . .

Though this looks killing, it leaves Black with a subtle defensive resource.

23	. . . .	KxB
24	Q—R6 ch	K—R1!
25	P—N6	. . . .

Despite all appearances to the contrary, Black can survive after 25 . . . BPxP; 26 PxP with 26 . . . R—B2!! as 27 RxR?? is ruled out because of 27 . . . Q—N7 mate.

After 27 PxR (best), the game might take the following difficult course: 27 . . . R—KB1; 28 Q—K6, Q—B4 ch; 29 R/1—B2!, BxR; 30 QxB, K—N2; 31 N—K4, Q—K6; 32 Q—N5 ch, QxQ ch; 33 NxQ, B—Q4; 34 R—Q2, BxBP; 35 NxB, RxN; 36 RxP, R—B2; 37 R—Q2 and White has good winning chances despite his doubled Pawn.

25	. . . .	Q—B4 ch?

This plausible move loses because Black has given up his mating threat.

26	R/1—B2!	BPxP
27	PxP	. . . .

Here, 27 . . . R—B2 will not do because of 28 RxR. Now we see the fatal damage wrought by Black's faulty 25th move.

27	. . . .	Q—N4 ch

Black must lose the exchange to stop mate.

28	QxQ	BxQ
29	RxR ch	RxR
30	RxR ch	K—N2
31	PxP	Resigns

For after 31 . . . KxP; 32 R—B7 ch wins easily for White. An exciting game.

30 *SICILIAN DEFENSE*

ROSENWALD TOURNAMENT / NEW YORK / 1957–58

The modern masters are so well acquainted with the fine points of opening analysis that it becomes desirable from time to time to take them "out of the books." The purpose is best served by adopting a noncommittal line which leaves room for maneuvering, regrouping, and meandering without giving the opponent a concrete hint of what is to come.

	White	*Black*
	FISCHER	FEUERSTEIN
1	P—K4	P—QB4
2	N—KB3	P—K3
3	P—KN3	. . . .

A favorite line of Fischer's. The idea is to play the King's Indian Defense with a move in hand.

3	. . . .	N—KB3
4	P—Q3	P—Q4
5	QN—Q2	B—K2
6	B—N2	Castles
7	Castles	N—B3
8	R—K1	. . . .

Because White intends to play P—K5 sooner or later, he provides ample protection for his King Pawn.

8 . . . . Q—B2
9 Q—K2 R—Q1

Black seems embarked on a policy of systematically massing his pieces on the Queen-side and neglecting the protection of his King. Simple development by 9 . . . B—Q2 (or 9 . . . P—QN3 and 10 . . . B—N2) was in order.

10 P—K5 N—K1

Now Black is ready to free his game a bit with . . . N—Q5. White's reply prevents this Knight move and also prepares for P—Q4.

11 P—B3 P—QN4

DIAGRAM 36 Position after 11 . . . P—QN4

Black (FEUERSTEIN)

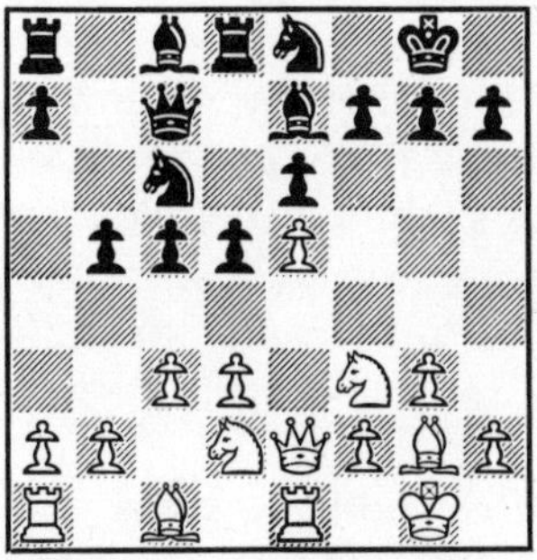

White (FISCHER)

The strategy on both sides is clearly marked out. White will try to attack on the King-side, helped by the fact that his powerful King Pawn prevents Black from posting a defensive piece on the important KB3 square. Black will try to open a line for counterattack on the Queen-side by . . . P—N5.

Since White's target is the Black King, his prospects for success are that much greater.

12	N—B1	P—N5
13	B—B4	....

A difficult decision. He can also play 13 P—B4, giving up control of his Q4 square but preventing Black from opening the Queen Knight file. After 13 P—B4, B—R3! Black would have fair chances.

13	....	Q—R4?!

Undoubtedly 13 . . . PxP; 14 PxP, R—N1 was the most straightforward continuation. But the actual move is not so bad as has been claimed.

14	P—B4!?	....

White prevents the opening of the Queen Knight file and also asserts his pressure on the long diagonal. Making his Q4 square accessible to the Black pieces seems a comparatively small price to pay for these advantages.

14	....	N—B2?

Withdrawing still another piece from the King-side. Comparatively better was 14 . . . N—Q5; for if 15 NxN, PxN; 16 PxP, PxP Black's clumsy doubled and isolated Queen Pawns are compensated for by his greater freedom of action and his command of key squares in the center.

15	P—KR4!	....

White on the other hand has his wits about him. The idea is to advance this Pawn to the sixth rank, creating a serious weakness on Black's black King-side squares. On the other hand, if Black limits this advance by . . . P—KR3 here or later, he creates a target for White's King-side attack: White can subsequently prepare a sacrifice by BxRP, or he can open the King Knight file with P—N4—5.

DIAGRAM 37 Position after 15 P—KR4!

Black (FEUERSTEIN)

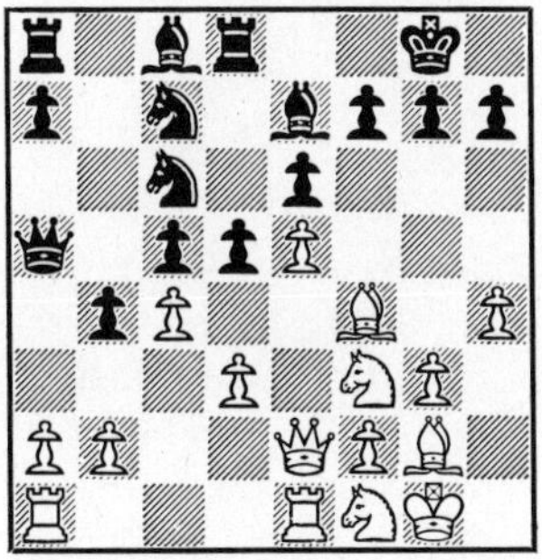

White (FISCHER)

15	....	Q—N3
16	P—R5	P—N6

Black's plan is to play . . . QPxP, leaving White with an artificially isolated Queen Bishop Pawn which cannot be guarded by P—N3. Black carries out this plan successfully by winning the weakened Pawn. But meanwhile White successfully executes his plan on the other wing.

17	P—R3	PxP
18	PxP	B—R3
19	N/1—R2!	....

This Knight is headed for KN4 and—eventually—KB6.

19	....	QR—B1

Black readies . . . N—Q5. The struggle of conflicting strategies becomes progressively more tense.

20	P—R6!	P—N3
21	B—N5!	....

With this possibility: 21 . . . BxB; 22 NxB, N—Q5; 23 Q—K3, N—B7; 24 Q—B4 (threatens mate), R—B1; 25 N—N4!, NxKR; 26 N—B6 ch, K—R1; 27 N—Q7 and

Black is lost, as White threatens not only 28 NxQ but chiefly 28 Q—B6 ch and 29 Q—N7 mate.

The following play now centers about White's relentless pressure on the black squares and the resulting mating potentialities.

21	....	N—Q5
22	Q—K3!	....

Stronger than 22 NxN, BxB etc.

White does not fear 22 . . . N—B7; 23 Q—B4, BxB; 24 NxB, which transposes into the variation given in the note to White's 21st move.

22	....	BxB
23	QxB	....

And now White does not fear 23 . . . N—B7 because of 24 KR—Q1!

And on 23 . . . BxP White continues his attack with 24 N—N4 etc.

23	....	N—K1
24	N—N4!	....

Now the threat is 25 N—B6 ch, K—R1; 26 NxN with a view to 27 Q—B6 ch and 28 Q—N7 mate.

24	....	N—B4

This Knight is an important bulwark, but sooner or later White will drive it away by advancing his King Knight Pawn.

25	QR—B1	Q—B2
26	N—Q2	R—Q5
27	NxP	RxP
28	QR—Q1	....

A new advantage for White: control of the Queen file.

28	....	R—R5

Or 28 . . . Q—K2; 29 QxQ, NxQ; 30 N—K3, R—QR5; 31 R—Q7 with an easy end game win for White.

29	R—K4!	....

White is now on the point of dislodging the enemy Knight from KB4. For example: 29 . . . RxR; 30 BxR threatening 31 BxN, KPxB; 32 N—B6 ch, K—R1; 33 NxN and wins.

29	....	B—N4
30	R—QB1	....

White steps up the pressure by menacing the Queen Bishop Pawn as well.

30	....	Q—N3
31	N—Q2	RxR
32	NxR	....

DIAGRAM 38 Position after 32 NxR

Black (FEUERSTEIN)

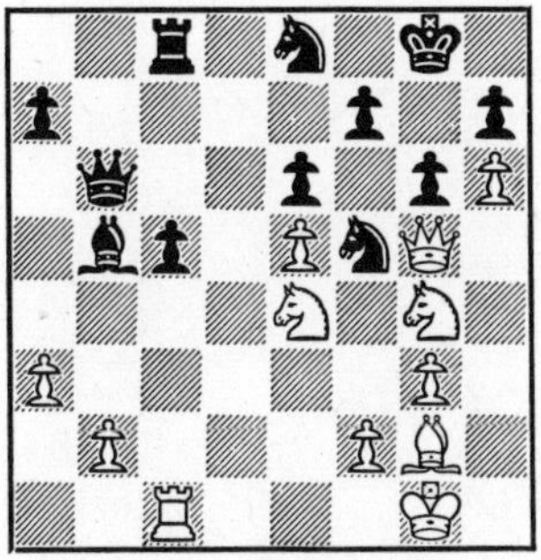

White (FISCHER)

Black can ward off the potential mating threats with 32 . . . Q—Q1 but after 33 QxQ, RxQ; 34 RxP the ending is hopeless for him.

32	....	B—Q6
33	N/N4—B6 ch	K—R1

Or 33 . . . NxN; 34 NxN ch, K—R1; 35 P—KN4!, N—Q5; 36 N—K4!, Q—Q1; 37 RxP! and Black is lost, for if 37 . . . BxN; 38 RxR wins.

34	P—KN4!	. . . .

The knockout blow, for if 34 . . . N—Q5; 35 NxN threatens 36 Q—B6 ch and 37 Q—N7 mate.

34	. . . .	BxN
35	BxB	N—Q5
36	NxN	Q—Q1

Black's last hope. After 37 QxQ, RxQ he hopes to recover the piece because of his threat of . . . N—K7 ch.

37	QxQ	RxQ
38	N—Q6!	. . . .

Very neat.

38	. . . .	N—K7 ch
39	K—B1	NxR

Or 39 . . . RxN; 40 PxR, NxR; 41 P—Q7 and White forces mate.

40	NxP ch	K—N1
41	NxR	N—N6
42	K—K2	N—Q5 ch
43	K—Q3	K—B1
44	N—B6	Resigns

Naturally White has an easy win. This fascinating game is notable for White's unruffled timing of his attacking moves.

31 *SICILIAN DEFENSE*

ROSENWALD TOURNAMENT / NEW YORK / 1957–58

Second Brilliancy Prize

In recent years the policy of countering the Sicilian Defense with highly speculative gambits has come to the fore. One such is seen in this game. Is it good or bad? On the basis of the play here, we cannot say.

	White	*Black*
	FISCHER	SHERWIN
1	P—K4	P—QB4
2	N—KB3	P—Q3
3	P—Q4	PxP
4	NxP	N—KB3
5	N—QB3	P—QR3
6	B—QB4	....

The usual move is 6 B—K2. The actual move may involve the sacrifice of a Pawn—but White is fully prepared for that possibility.

6	....	P—K3
7	Castles!?	....

White's more prudent course is 7 P—QR4 (preventing . . . P—QN4) or 7 P—QR3 (preventing . . . P—N5 as a follow-up to 7 . . . P—QN4).

7	....	P—QN4
8	B—N3	....

White can save his Pawn with 8 B—Q3, but this would be a confession that 6 B—QB4 was waste of time.

8	....	P—N5
9	N—N1	....

DIAGRAM 39 Position after 9 N—N1

Black (SHERWIN)

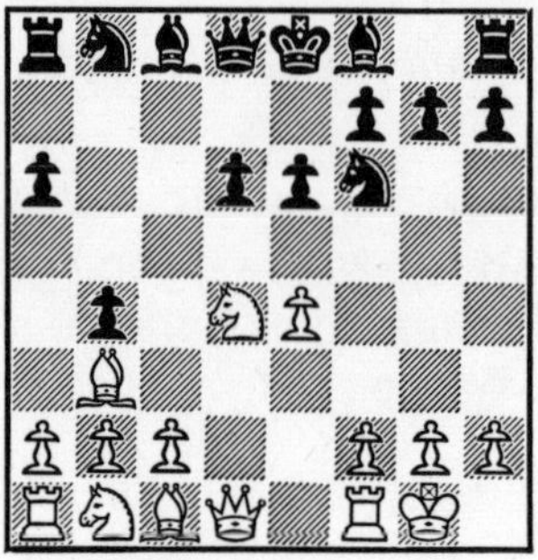

White (FISCHER)

9	....	B—Q2

Black is irresolute. It seems that after 9 . . . NxP; 10 Q—B3, P—Q4 (or 10 . . . B—N2), Black is reasonably safe.

10	B—K3	....

White persists in offering the nebulous gambit.

10	....	N—B3

And once more Black prudently refrains.

11	P—KB3	....

Playing it safe after all.

11	....	B—K2
12	P—B3!	....

So Black's 8 . . . P—N5 turns out to be a liability after all. Because 12 . . . P—QR4; 13 N—N5, Q—N1; 14 P—QR4 would leave Black with a most uncomfortable game, Black is virtually forced to capture.

12	....	PxP
13	NxN	....

A trap. If Black tries the tempting 13 . . . PxP?; 14 NxQ, PxR/Q White wins the second Queen with 15 B—Q4.

13	....	BxN
14	NxP	....

White has a majority of two Pawns to one on the Queen-side, which may turn out to be an endgame advantage. In addition, it is not unlikely that Black's Queen Rook Pawn may become difficult to defend.

14	....	Castles
15	R—B1!	Q—N1?

A questionable move. Instead, 15 . . . B—N2 was safer.

16	N—Q5!	....

This alert move gives White the advantage. A plausible possibility here is 16 . . . BxN; 17 PxB, NxP; 18 BxN, PxB; 19 P—QN3, Q—N4; 20 Q—Q2 and White will regain the Pawn advantageously by playing a Rook to the Queen file.

16	....	PxN
17	RxB	PxP
18	PxP	....

White is left with a weak King Pawn, but he has more than enough compensation in his Bishop-pair and in the open lines for his Rooks.

DIAGRAM 40 Position after 18 PxP

Black (SHERWIN)

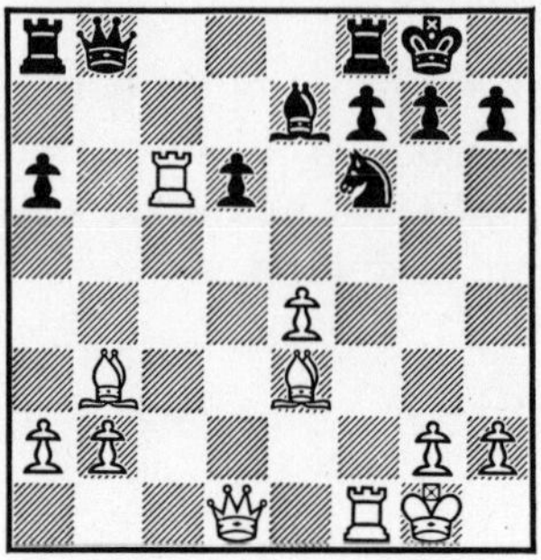

White (FISCHER)

Against 18 . . . NxP White has the winning reply 19 RxBP!, RxR; 20 Q—Q5! etc.

18	. . . .	Q—N4
19	R—N6	Q—K4
20	B—Q4!	Q—KN4

The shaky-looking King Pawn is immune (20 . . . QxKP?; 21 R—K1).

21	Q—B3	N—Q2
22	R—N7	N—K4
23	Q—K2	B—B3

Black threatens to simplify drawishly with . . . N—B6 ch followed by . . . BxB ch.

24	K—R1	P—QR4

The days of this weak Pawn are numbered.

25	B—Q5	. . . .

White threatens—if nothing better offers—to win a Pawn with 26 BxN, PxB (not 26 . . . QxB?; 27 R—N5 threatening BxR as well as BxP ch); 27 RxP etc.

25	....	QR—B1
26	B—B3	....

Preventing . . . R—B8 and at the same time menacing Black's Queen Rook Pawn, which can no longer be held.

26	....	P—R5
27	R—R7	N—N5

Black works hard for simplification. White falls in with his plans—at a price.

28	RxRP!	BxB
29	PxB	RxP

The stage is set for a remarkable combination.

DIAGRAM 41 Position after 29 . . . RxP

Black (SHERWIN)

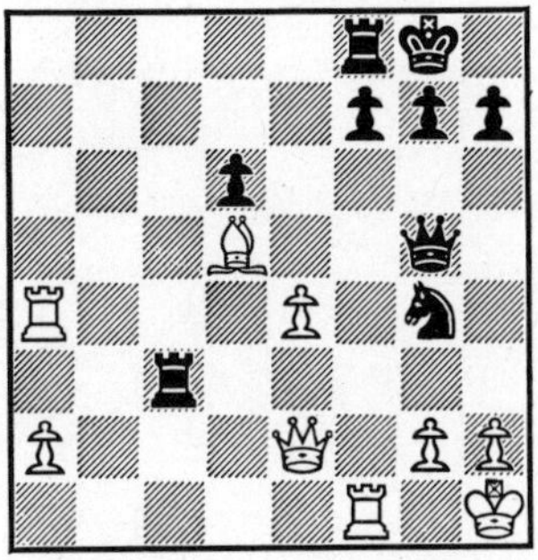

White (FISCHER)

30	RxP!!	....

A beautiful move, finely calculated. If Black replies 30 . . . RxR?? White forces mate with 31 R—R8 ch etc.

Nor will 30 . . . QxB do because of 31 RxR ch! (not 31 PxQ??, R—B8 ch and Black forces mate), KxR; 32 Q—B1 ch!, Q—B2; 33 R—R8 ch, K—K2; 34 R—R7 ch winning the Black Queen.

30	....	R—B8 ch

Black has an ingenious try here in 30 . . . P—R4?!

One possibility (after 30 . . . P—R4?!) is 31 R—B1 dis ch, K—R2; 32 RxR, R—B8 ch; 33 R—B1, Q—B5! and the double mating threat wins for Black.

Also possible after 30 . . . P—R4?! is 31 R—B3 dis ch, K—R2; 32 RxR/B3, N—B7 ch; 33 K—N1, N—R6 ch and Black has a draw by perpetual check.

However, after 30 . . . P—R4?! White intended 31 RxR dbl ch!, KxR; 32 Q—B1 ch, N—B3; 33 R—B4, RxR; 34 QxR, NxB; 35 PxN and the slow but sure advance of White's Queen Rook Pawn wins for him.

31	Q—B1!	....

This is the move that upsets Black's calculations: he had expected 31 R—B1 dis ch?, K—R1; 32 R—R8, RxR/R1; 33 BxR, Q—B5! and White is lost.

31	....	P—R4

Too late Black realizes that 31 . . . RxQ ch; 32 RxR dis ch wins easily for White (32 . . . R—B2; 33 R—R8 ch and mate next move—or 32 . . . QxB; 33 RxR ch and wins).

32	QxR!	....

Another ingratiating point: after 32 . . . QxQ ch; 33 R—B1 dis ch White winds up a Rook ahead.

32	....	Q—R5
33	RxR dbl ch	K—R2
34	P—KR3	Q—N6
35	PxN	P—R5
36	B—K6	Resigns

White played all phases of this taxing game with amazing aplomb.

32 *KING'S FIANCHETTO*

ROSENWALD TOURNAMENT / NEW YORK / 1957–58

Many players experience psychological difficulties when they have to play against an opening variation of which they are fond. Fischer is quite untroubled, however, when an opponent adopts an opening favored by Bobby.

	White	*Black*
	KRAMER	FISCHER
1	N—KB3	N—KB3
2	P—KN3	P—KN3
3	B—N2	....

This colorless opening is cruelly boring for a player of mercurial temperament. However, Fischer seems to thrive on it.

3	....	B—N2
4	Castles	Castles
5	P—Q3	P—Q3
6	P—K4	P—B4

With this move Black departs from symmetry and sets up a Sicilian Defense of sorts. In keeping with the Sicilian theme, White could now play 7 N—B3 with a fair game.

DIAGRAM 42 Position after 6 . . . P—B4

Black (FISCHER)

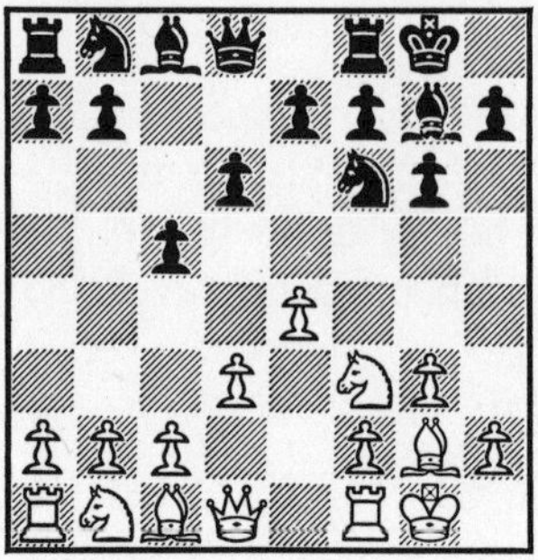

White (KRAMER)

7	P—B3?	. . . .

But this is definitely a strategic blunder, on which Black fastens his attention with a skill that is really masterly. White's Queen Bishop Pawn has become a target along the long diagonal; this calls for . . . P—QN4—5 to heighten the power of the fianchettoed diagonal.

7	. . . .	N—B3
8	N—K1	. . . .

White makes way for the advance of his King Bishop Pawn in order to start a demonstration on the King-side. But this is of no great moment, and what really matters is that White has no prospects of achieving an effective development.

8	. . . .	R—N1!

Preparing for the coming advance of his Queen Knight Pawn.

9	P—KB4	N—K1

Black unmasks the diagonal of his fianchettoed Bishop as he prepares to carry out his grand plan. In addition this

Knight—unlike his White counterpart at K1—will play a very useful role on the Queen-side.

10 B—K3 ....

White's best hope is to create a diversion on the King-side by means of a Pawn-storming attack: P—B5 followed by P—KN4 etc.

DIAGRAM 43 Position after 10 B—K3

Black (FISCHER)

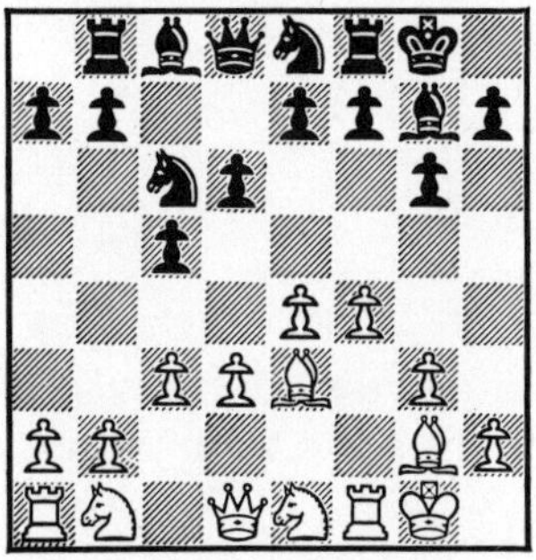

White (KRAMER)

One would now expect 10 . . . P—QN4 but then, after 11 P—Q4!, PxP; 12 PxP, White has a game of sorts, as 12 . . . Q—N3 is effectively answered by 13 N—B2 threatening P—Q5.

10 .... B—Q2!

A clever waiting move. The point is that 10 P—Q4? can be answered by 10 . . . PxP; 11 PxP, Q—N3! and now that Black's Queen is not masked by his Queen Knight Pawn, Black wins a Pawn.

11 N—Q2 P—QN4!

Now this move is in order.

12 P—K5 ....

Hoping to open up the game for his Bishops, he succeeds only in opening up the game for the *Black* Bishops.

12	....	PxP
13	BxP	PxP
14	RxP	N—B2

A useful gain of time, . . . N—K3 being threatened.

15	R—KB1	P—N5!

Black has carried out his plan satisfactorily. The reply 16 PxP allows 16 . . . BxP, after which Black has a completely open long diagonal and White's Queen Pawn is pitiably weak.

16	Q—B2	PxP
17	PxP	N—N4!
18	P—Q4	....

Instead of blocking the diagonal of Black's sinister Bishop, this merely creates a new target.

18	....	R—B1!

Intensifying the pressure. Black threatens to win with 19 . . . NxBP!; 20 QxN, NxP (threatening . . . N—K7 ch, and . . . N—K3 for good measure), or with 19 . . . N/B3xP!; 20 PxN, BxP ch; 21 BxB, RxQ; 22 NxR, NxB; 23 NxN, Q—N3; 24 N/Q2—B3, P—K4 and wins.

DIAGRAM 44 Position after 18 . . . R—B1!

Black (FISCHER)

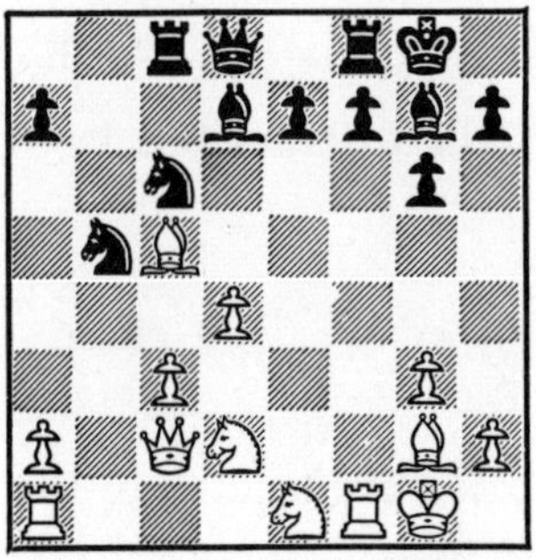

White (KRAMER)

In reply to 19 R—B1, Fischer later gave 19 . . . N/B3xP!; 20 PxN, BxP ch; 21 BxB, NxB (another way is 21 . . . RxQ; 22 NxR, NxB; 23 NxN, Q—N3 as previously shown); 22 Q—Q3, RxR; 23 QxN, B—N4!; 24 Q—N2, Q—N3 ch; 25 K—R1, BxR; 26 QxR, BxB ch; 27 NxB, R—Q1 and Black wins quickly.

19	Q—N2	NxBP!

Decisive.

20	QxN	NxP
21	Q—N4	. . . .

Or 21 QxN, BxQ ch; 22 BxB, B—N4 and Black wins more material.

21	. . . .	N—K7 ch

If now 22 K—B2, RxB!; 23 KxN (not 23 QxR, B—Q5 ch), R—QN4 and Black wins easily.

22	K—R1	RxB
23	QxR	. . . .

On 23 QR—N1 Black has a neat turn in 23 . . . R—KR4! threatening . . . NxP ch as well as . . . B—B6.

23	....	BxR
24	N/K1—B3	B—N2
25	R—K1	N—B6

White can now win a Pawn but he will still remain a Pawn down.

26	QxRP	B—K3
27	P—QR3	Q—Q3
28	Q—R5	B—Q4

While White's forces are scattered, Black's cooperate relentlessly. Black threatens 29 . . . R—R1; 30 Q—N4, RxP. White avoids this—only to lose a piece.

29	N—QN1?	R—R1
30	Q—N4	QxQ
31	PxQ	BxN!

If now 32 BxB, R—R8 wins the piece.

32	NxN	....

Probably expecting 32 . . . BxN?; 33 BxB!

32	....	BxB ch!
	Resigns	

An exceedingly well-played game by Black: impeccable strategy backed up by many ingenious tactical points.

33 *SICILIAN DEFENSE*

INTERZONAL TOURNAMENT / PORTOROZ / 1958

Since Fischer is so fond of playing the Sicilian Defense when he has the Black pieces, it is always interesting to see how he proceeds against this defense when he has the White pieces.

	White	*Black*
	FISCHER	LARSEN
1	P—K4	P—QB4
2	N—KB3	P—Q3
3	P—Q4	PxP
4	NxP	N—KB3
5	N—QB3	P—KN3
6	B—K3	B—N2

White wants to play Q—Q2 which, if played at once, can be answered with . . . N—KN5. The usual way to prevent the Knight move is B—K2 but White intends to play B—QB4. This explains his next move.

7	P—B3	Castles
8	Q—Q2	N—B3

In the event of 9 Castles, Black has reasonable counter-attacking chances after 9 . . . NxN; 10 BxN, B—K3; 11 K—N1, P—QR3; 12 P—KR4, P—QN4 etc.

9	B—QB4	NxN
10	BxN	B—K3

Black naturally strives to eliminate the effectiveness of White's King Bishop. The exchange by 11 BxB, PxB would be useful for Black, as an eventual N—Q5 would be out of the question.

11	B—N3	Q—R4
12	Castles/Q	P—QN4
13	K—N1	. . . .

DIAGRAM 45 Position after 13 K—N1

Black (LARSEN)

White (FISCHER)

As is true of almost all positions where the players have castled on opposite wings, an exciting game is in prospect. White will advance his Pawns on the King-side, Black on the other wing.

Meanwhile White threatens to win a Pawn with 14 N—Q5!

13	....	P—N5
14	N—Q5	BxN
15	BxB	....

After 15 PxB, Q—N4 the position of White's King Bishop becomes uncomfortable in view of the possibility of . . . P—QR4—5.

15	....	QR—B1

After this White maintains a very strong attack. The lesser evil was 15 . . . NxB; 16 PxN (on 16 BxB Black gets good chances with 16 . . . N—B6 ch!), QxQP; 17 QxP and White has the edge.

16	B—N3	R—B2

Black's coming demonstration on the Queen Bishop file is meaningless. On the other hand, White's prospective opening of the King Rook file is packed with potential menace.

17 P—KR4! Q—QN4

Black wants to play . . . P—QR4—5, but somehow he never gets the time to do so.

18 P—R5! . . . .

DIAGRAM 46 Position after 18 P—R5!

Black (LARSEN)

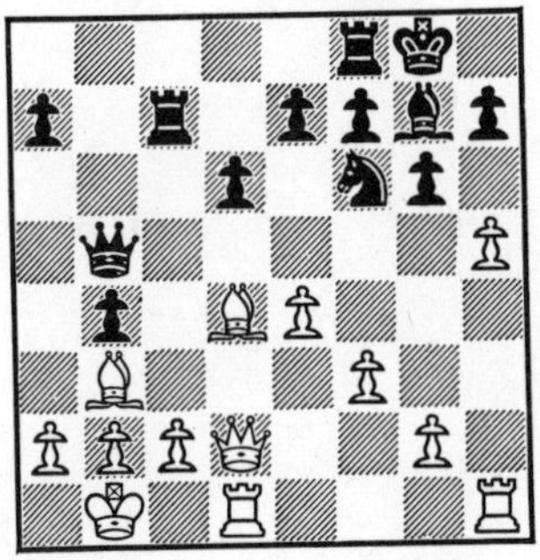

White (FISCHER)

White pursues the attack with great energy. A characteristic possibility now is 18 . . . NxRP; 19 BxB, KxB; 20 P—N4, N—B3; 21 Q—R6 ch, K—N1; 22 P—N5, N—R4; 23 RxN, PxR; 24 P—N6!, RPxP; 25 QxNP ch, and White mates rapidly. Note the power of his King Bishop, which will be documented in the coming play as well.

18 . . . . KR—B1
19 PxP RPxP
20 P—N4! P—R4

Threatening . . . P—R5. The game has now reached its most critical stage.

21 P—N5! . . . .

If Black tries 21 . . . N—K1, the Tournament Book shows a win with 22 BxB, NxB; 23 R—R6! winning in all variations, for example:

I 23 . . . P—R5; 24 Q—R2, N—R4; 25 RxP ch, K—B1; 26 QxN and wins.

II 23 . . . P—K3; 24 QxQP, P—R5; 25 QR—R1, N—R4; 26 BxKP!, PxB; 27 QxKP ch and wins.

III 23 . . . Q—K4; 24 QR—R1, N—R4; 25 RxP ch and wins.

21	....	N—R4
22	RxN!	PxR

No better is 22 . . . BxB; 23 QxB, PxR; 24 P—N6, P—K3; 25 QxQP etc.

23	P—N6	....

Here too the powerful diagonal of White's King Bishop is the deciding factor.

DIAGRAM 47 Position after 23 P—N6

Black (LARSEN)

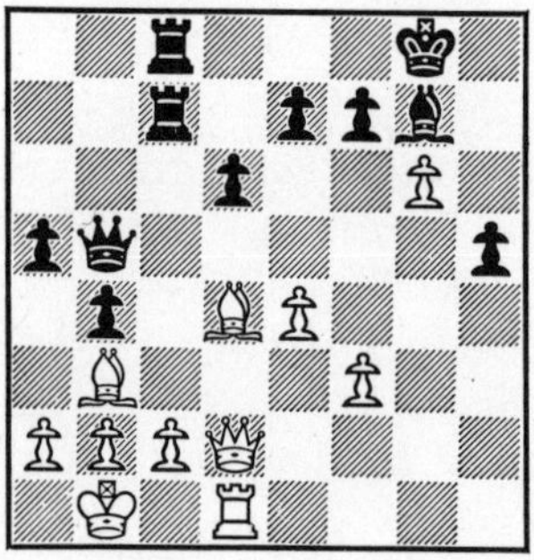

White (FISCHER)

The attempt to break the diagonal with 23 . . . P—K3 will not do because of 24 PxP ch, RxKBP (if 24 . . . KxP; 25 Q—B4 ch! wins); 25 BxP and White wins.

Or if 23 . . . BxB; 24 Q—R6!, B—N2; 25 Q—R7 ch, K—B1; 26 PxP, P—K3; 27 R—N1!, Q—K4; 28 Q—N8 ch, K—K2; 29 RxB! and wins.

23	....	P—K4
24	PxP ch	K—B1
25	B—K3	....

Threatening QxQP ch or 26 B—R6.

25	....	P—Q4

Black is fishing in troubled waters. He hopes for 26 BxP, RxP with some counterplay.

26	PxP	....

A very strong passed Pawn. The reply 26 . . . P—R5 is smartly countered by 27 P—Q6!

26	....	RxKBP
27	P—Q6	R—KB3

Giving up the defense of the second rank loses quickly. However, after 27 . . . R—Q2 there are various winning lines, the simplest being 28 B—K6 and the strongest probably 28 Q—R2.

28	B—N5!	Q—N2

Hopeless, but if he tries 28 . . . R—N3 there follows 29 B—K7 ch, K—K1; 30 P—Q7 ch etc.

29	BxR	BxB
30	P—Q7	R—Q1

DIAGRAM 48 Position after 30 . . . R—Q1

Black (LARSEN)

White (FISCHER)

According to some magazine versions White played 31 Q—Q6 ch and Black resigned, as mate is in the offing.

However, according to the official version in the Tournament Book, White played an even stronger move:

31	Q—R6 ch	Resigns

For if 31 . . . K—K2; 32 Q—R7 ch and mate next move. Or 31 . . . B—N2; 32 Q—Q6 mate. A very rewarding game, and Fischer's best in this very formidable event.

34 *RUY LOPEZ*

INTERZONAL TOURNAMENT / PORTOROZ / 1958

The popular conception about drawn games is that they are all dull. Many are, to be sure, but there are happy exceptions. In this game White plays colorlessly and allows his opponent to get a very strong position. When the crisis arrives, White stages a magnificent fight to stave off disaster. The well contested draw is a legitimate outcome.

	White	*Black*
	FISCHER	SZABO
1	P—K4	P—K4
2	N—KB3	N—QB3
3	B—N5	P—QR3
4	B—R4	N—B3
5	Castles	B—K2
6	R—K1	P—QN4
7	B—N3	Castles

DIAGRAM 49 Position after 7 . . . Castles

Black (SZABO)

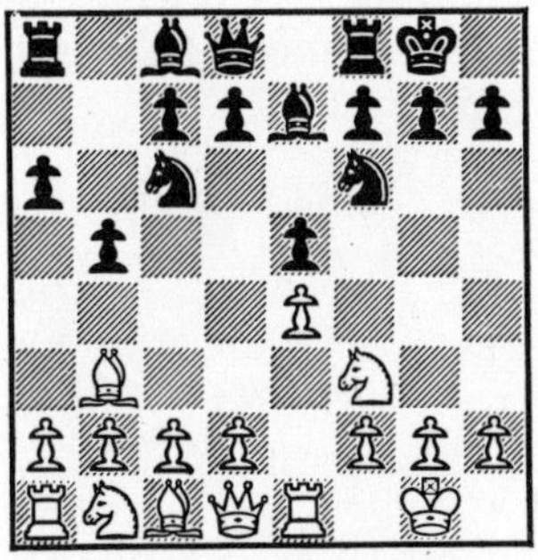

White (FISCHER)

Black's last move (instead of the more usual 7 . . . P—Q3) is a hint that he intends to play the feared Marshall Attack after 8 P—B3: 8 . . . P—Q4!?; 9 PxP, NxP; 10 NxP, NxN; 11 RxN, N—B3 followed by 12 . . . B—Q3 with a very aggressive position in return for the Pawn sacrifice.

To avoid this uncomfortable line of play, White chooses a colorless reply.

8	P—KR3	B—N2
9	P—B3	P—Q4!?

A man with a one-track mind: he is determined to offer a gambit.

10	PxP	NxP
11	P—Q3	....

White plays safe by declining the gambit, but he is left with a difficult game anyway.

11	....	Q—Q3
12	QN—Q2	QR—Q1!

With unerring eye Black concentrates on the weak Queen Pawn.

13	N—K4	Q—N3
14	N—N3	....

This allows a very powerful reply, but it is not clear that White has anything better. Even at this early stage the completion of his development shapes up as a difficult if not insoluble problem.

14	....	B—B4!

Thanks to White's early advance of his King Rook Pawn, Black now threatens 15 . . . QxN. If White plays 15 N—K4, Black can reply 15 . . . B—N3 with a very strong game. How then is White to continue?

DIAGRAM 50 Position after 14 . . . B—B4!

Black (SZABO)

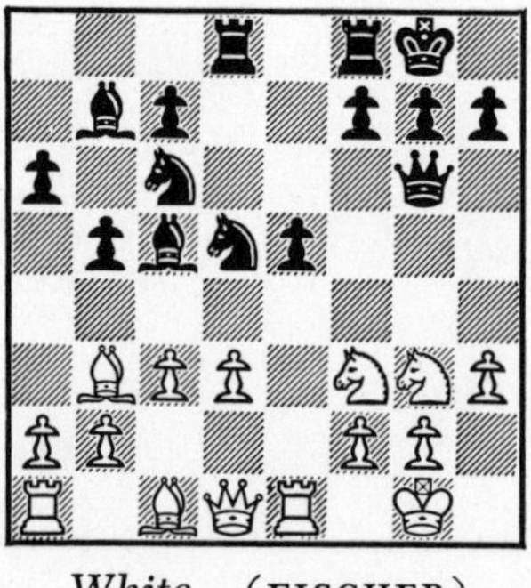

White (FISCHER)

15	P—Q4!	....

A very risky but very formidable move. Suddenly it appears that White is threatening to open a dangerous attack by means of B—B2. However, Black has counterchances, so that the position becomes exceedingly critical for both players.

15	....	PxP
16	PxP	N/Q4—N5

Virtually forced. He tries to stave off White's B—B2.

17	B—K3	....

Threatening 18 P—R3, N—Q4; 19 B—B2 and wins. Black is left with no choice.

17	....	NxQP!
18	NxN	BxN
19	BxB	P—QB4

Apparently Black has extricated himself and now has a won game.

20	BxQBP!	....

The only move, and doubtless a long foreseen resource.

20	....	RxQ
21	QRxR	....

White has a Rook and Bishop for the Queen—a material minus—but he threatens to win at least the exhcange. If now 21 . . . N—B3; 22 BxR, KxB; 23 R—Q7 and White wins. Or if 21 . . . Q—QB3; 22 N—K4! wins.

21	....	N—Q6!

A trap: if White plays 22 B—B2? (anticipating 22 . . . R—Q1; 23 RxN! and wins, for if 23 . . . RxR??; 24 R—K8 mate), Black wins with 22 . . . Q—QB3! threatening . . . QxP mate.

DIAGRAM 51 Position after 21 . . . N—Q6!

Black (SZABO)

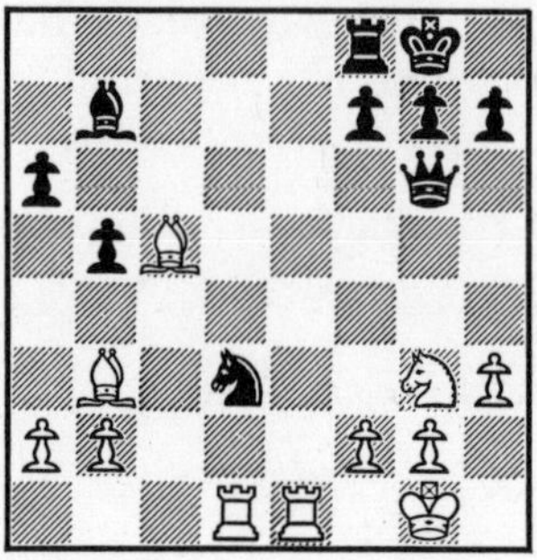

White (FISCHER)

22	BxR!	NxR
23	R—Q8!	P—KR4!

The only move. Black lifts the mate threat and holds the threat of . . . P—R5 (winning White's Knight) in reserve.

24	B—N4 dis ch	K—R2

Now 25 BxN is answered by 25 . . . P—R5.

25	R—Q6!	. . . .

Setting a neat trap: if 25 . . . P—B3?; 26 BxN, P—R5; 27 R—Q7, B—R1; 28 R—R7, B—B3; 29 R—QB7, B—R1; 30 B—B2 and White wins.

25	. . . .	Q—N8!

Threatening . . . N—B6 mate.

26	R—Q1	Q—N3

If White captures the Knight, Black regains the piece with . . . P—R5.

27	R—Q6	Q—N8!
28	R—Q1	Q—N3
29	RxN	P—R5

30	R—K3	PxN
31	RxP	Q—N8 ch
32	K—R2	Q—B4

But not 32 . . . QxNP?; 33 B—B3 and White wins.

33	K—N1	Drawn

A legitimate outcome. White cannot afford to hem in his Rook with P—B3, and must therefore agree to a draw by 33 . . . Q—N8 ch; 34 K—R2, Q—B4; 35 K—N1, Q—N8 ch etc. A beautifully contested game.

35 *SICILIAN DEFENSE*

UNITED STATES CHAMPIONSHIP (ROSENWALD TOURNAMENT) / 1958–59

In these days of relentless refurbishing of old opening variations the masters vie with each other in avid study of hidden fine points. This is one of Fischer's strongest qualities and one of Reshevsky's weakest. Hence the following game:

	White	*Black*
	FISCHER	RESHEVSKY
1	P—K4	P—QB4
2	N—KB3	N—QB3
3	P—Q4	PxP
4	NxP	P—KN3
5	N—QB3	. . . .

If White tries to get a strong bind on the Q5 square with 5 P—QB4, Black gets good counterplay with 5 . . . N—R3 followed by . . . P—B4.

5	. . . .	B—N2
6	B—K3	N—B3
7	B—QB4	. . . .

Fischer's favorite move against the Sicilian.

7 .... Castles

In the game Fischer-Panno at Portoroz in 1958, White played 8 P—B3?! allowing the embarrassing reply 8 . . . Q—N3! (threatens . . . QxP as well as . . . NxP!). After an hour and a half of intensive reflection Fischer found 9 B—N3!, NxP; 10 N—Q5! forcing 10 . . . Q—R4 ch; then, after 11 P—B3, N—B4; 12 NxN, QPxN; 13 NxP ch White recovered his Pawn and the game ended in an early draw.

Here Fischer improves on his play.

8 B—N3! ....

Black can now play 8 . . . P—Q3. Then after 9 P—B3 the play might follow on the lines of Fischer-Larsen (Game 33).

Instead, Reshevsky commits a fearful blunder.

DIAGRAM 52 Position after 8 B—N3!

Black (RESHEVSKY)

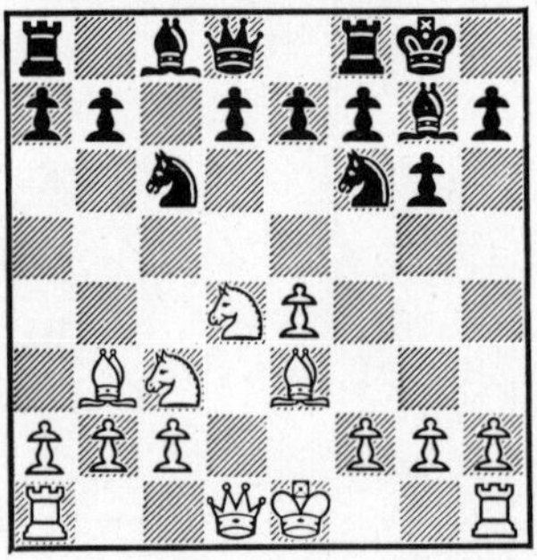

White (FISCHER)

8 .... N—QR4??

Reshevsky's adoption of this move reveals that he is blissfully unaware of earlier Russian analysis and games which supply the following moves.

9	P—K5!	N—K1

The only way to put up a fight, albeit a losing fight, is 9 . . . NxB; 10 KPxN, NxR; 11 PxB, NxP ch; 12 QxN and White has a winning advantage in material.

The actual move, incredible as it may seem, loses the Black Queen.

10	BxP ch!!	KxB

On 10 . . . RxB or 10 . . . K—R1 the same reply still confiscates Black's Queen.

11	N—K6!	PxN

Or 11 . . . KxN; 12 Q—Q5 ch, K—B4; 13 P—N4 ch and White mates in four moves at most.

12	QxQ	N—QB3

Since it would be disgraceful to resign at this point, Reshevsky struggles on for another thirty moves despite his crushing material disadvantage.

13	Q—Q2	BxP
14	Castles/K	N—Q3
15	B—B4	N—B5
16	Q—K2	BxB
17	QxN	K—N2
18	N—K4	. . . .

White now concentrates on winning Black's foremost King Pawn.

18	. . . .	B—B2
19	N—B5	R—B3
20	P—QB3	P—K4
21	QR—Q1	N—Q1
22	N—Q7	. . . .

Not 22 NxP because of 22 . . . R—B3.

22	. . . .	R—B3
23	Q—KR4	R—K3

24	N—B5	R—KB3
25	N—K4	....

The victorious conclusion to the Knight maneuver, 24 . . . R—K3 or . . . R—B2 being refuted by 25 N—N5.

25	....	R—B5
26	QxKP ch	R—B2
27	Q—R3	N—B3
28	N—Q6	BxN
29	RxB	B—B4
30	P—QN4!	R/B2—B1
31	P—N5	N—Q1
32	R—Q5	N—B2
33	R—B5	P—QR3
34	P—N6!	B—K5
35	R—K1	B—B3

DIAGRAM 53 Position after 35 . . . B—B3

Black (RESHEVSKY)

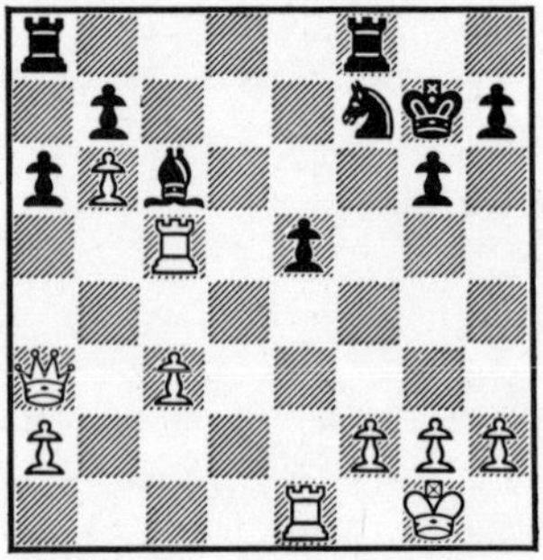

White (FISCHER)

36	RxB!	....

The quickest way. White relies on the resulting passed Pawn.

36	....	PxR
37	P—N7	QR—N1

38	QxP	N—Q1
39	R—N1	R—B2

Black can now win the advanced Pawn, but this leads to a clearly lost game.

40	P—KR3!	R/B2xNP
41	RxR	RxR

Or 41 . . . NxR; 42 Q—R7 and White wins a piece.

42	Q—R8	Resigns

At long last. After 42 . . . R—N8 ch; 43 K—R2, R—Q8; 44 P—QR4 Black is helpless against the further advance of the deadly passed Pawn.

36 *RUY LOPEZ*

MAR DEL PLATA / 1959

Though lacking sensational qualities, this is a game of a high order. White operates subtly with small advantages, and there are two features here that show the hand of a master: the simultaneous operations on both wings, and sly tactical points that support the general strategic plan.

	White	*Black*
	FISCHER	SHOCRON
1	P—K4	P—K4
2	N—KB3	N—QB3
3	B—N5	P—QR3
4	B—R4	N—B3
5	Castles	B—K2
6	R—K1	P—QN4
7	B—N3	Castles
8	P—B3	. . . .

This gives Black the opportunity of playing the dreaded Marshall Attack (see Game 34—Fischer-Szabo—on this point).

8	....	P—Q3

Black ducks the challenge after all and transposes into the orthodox line.

9	P—KR3	N—QR4
10	B—B2	P—B4
11	P—Q4	Q—B2
12	QN—Q2	B—Q2
13	N—B1	KR—K1
14	N—K3	P—N3

Black intends to play . . . B—KB1 followed by . . . B—N2. However, the actual move weakens his King-side black squares—a circumstance which Fischer exploits in masterly fashion. Hence 14 . . . B—KB1 was safer.

15	PxKP	....

As White intends to operate on the wings he first stabilizes the position in the center.

15	....	PxP
16	N—R2!	QR—Q1
17	Q—B3	B—K3
18	N/R2—N4	NxN

This opens the King Rook file for White and thus subjects Black to lasting pressure. The alternative 18 . . . N—Q2 is playable but not inviting.

19	PxN	Q—B3

If Black tries to forestall White's next move with 19 . . . B—N4? White wins the exchange with 20 N—Q5!

DIAGRAM 54 Position after 19 . . . Q—B3

Black (SHOCRON)

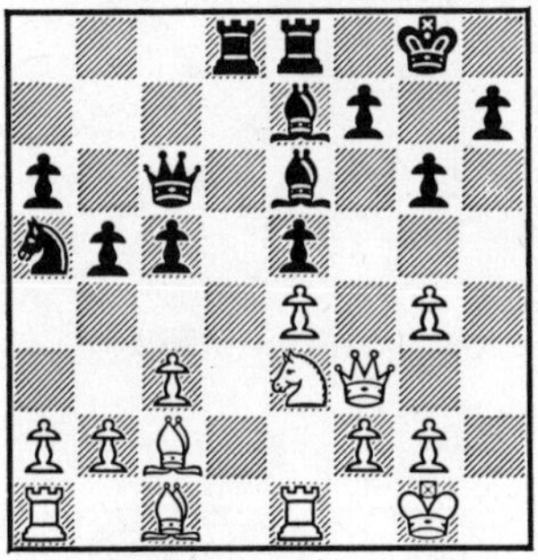

White (FISCHER)

20	P—N5!	. . . .

This surprising move cannot very well be answered by 20 . . . BxNP, for then White still wins the exchange with 21 N—Q5!, BxB (much worse is 21 . . . B—K2?; 22 NxB ch, RxN; 23 Q—B6 and White wins because of the double threat of 24 B—R6 and 24 QxR—a fine example of how to exploit the black-square weakness); 22 N—B6 ch and 23 NxR.

20	. . . .	N—B5
21	N—N4!	BxN

Else White forces the removal of the other Bishop with N—B6 ch. But now White is left with the two Bishops against Bishop and Knight. The Bishops will become ominously active as soon as White has succeeded in opening up the position.

22	QxB	N—N3

Black must now lose considerable time to bring this Knight to the KB1 square to guard against White's threat to occupy the open King Rook file with Queen and Rook.

23	P—KN3	P—B5
24	K—N2	N—Q2
25	R—R1	N—B1

The Knight now guards Black's King Rook Pawn adequately, but this piece has little scope. White therefore must think about opening up the game. Here 26 P—R4 looks logical, but Black has a good reply in 26 . . . P—N5.

DIAGRAM 55 Position after 25 . . . N—B1

Black (SHOCRON)

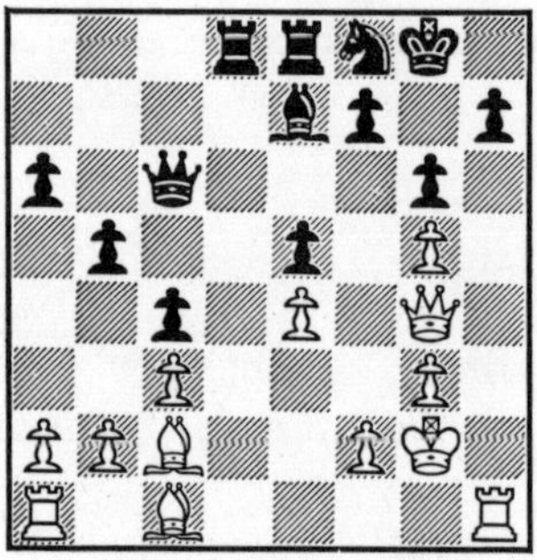

White (FISCHER)

26	P—N4!	. . . .

Once more White resorts to a Pawn sacrifice, this time on the other wing. The idea is that after 26 . . . PxP *e.p.*; 27 BxP, QxBP; 28 B—K3 White has a strong attack. One threat, pointed out by Kmoch, is 29 Q—B3!, N—K3; 30 BxN, PxB; 31 RxP!, R—KB1; 32 QR—R1!!, RxQ; 33 R—R8 ch and 34 R/R1—R7 mate.

26	. . . .	Q—K3
27	Q—K2	. . . .

Now White threatens to open the Queen Rook file effectively with 28 P—R4. Black forestalls him—so he thinks—but he is really meeting White halfway.

27	....	P—QR4
28	PxP	Q—R3
29	B—K3	QxP
30	P—R4!	....

Beginning the decisive line-opening. On 30 . . . PxP White wins the exchange with 31 BxP! and on 30 . . . P—N5; 31 PxP, QxNP; 32 KR—QN1, Q—B6; 33 P—R5 White's passed Pawn is much more menacing than Black's.

30	....	R—R1
31	PxP!	....

For after 31 . . . QxR; 32 RxQ, RxR; 33 QxP White's passed Pawns would win easily for him.

31	....	QxNP
32	KR—QN1	....

Now White has the open lines he was seeking and his advantage grows rapidly.

32	....	Q—B3
33	R—N6!	....

Here too Black can try to get two Rooks for his Queen with 33 . . . QxR; 34 BxQ, RxR, though in that case 35 QxP should win without too much trouble. Another way after 33 . . . QxR would be 34 RxR, Q—QB3; 35 RxR, QxR; 36 QxP etc.

33	....	Q—B2
34	R/N6—R6!	....

This assures White's control of the Queen Rook file, with further inroads to come.

34	....	RxR
35	RxR	R—B1
36	Q—N4	....

Suddenly the scene of action begins to shift to the center and King-side. White's immediate threat is 37 R—R7, Q—Q1; 38 RxB etc.

36	....	N—K3
37	B—R4!	R—N1
38	R—B6!	Q—Q1

This allows a quick decision, but on 38 . . . Q—Q2 White wins with 39 RxP etc.

DIAGRAM 56 Position after 38 . . . Q—Q1

Black (SHOCRON)

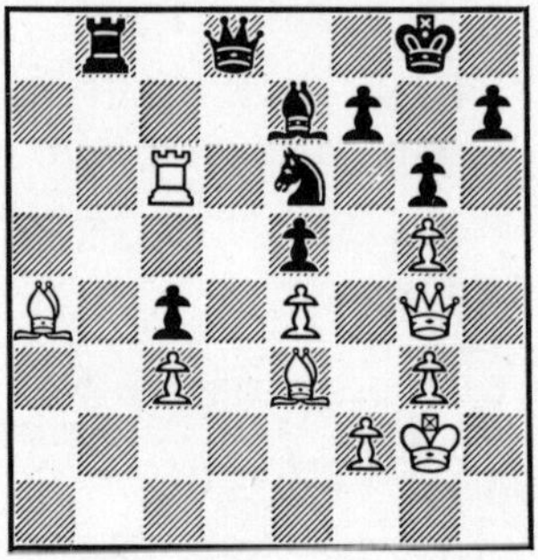

White (FISCHER)

39	RxN!	....

An unexpected but quite logical stroke. The idea is 39 . . . PxR; 40 QxP ch, K—B1; 41 QxKP and White must win, for example 41 . . . K—B2; 42 B—Q4, Q—KB1; 43 B—Q7, R—Q1; 44 B—K6 ch, K—K1; 45 Q—N5 ch and mate next move.

39	....	Q—QB1
40	B—Q7!	Resigns

A beautiful finishing touch: if 40 . . . QxB; 41 RxNP ch etc. White's grand strategy has been very impressive.

37 *SICILIAN DEFENSE*

MAR DEL PLATA / 1959

Sometimes Fischer's games remind us of those of Reshevsky. Both players are masters of the art of springing elegant surprises in barren-looking positions.

	White	*Black*
	PILNIK	FISCHER
1	P—K4	P—QB4
2	N—KB3	P—Q3
3	P—Q4	PxP
4	NxP	N—KB3
5	N—QB3	P—QR3
6	B—K2	P—K4

A very popular variation in recent years despite the fact that it leaves Black with a backward Queen Pawn.

7	N—N3	B—K2
8	Castles	Castles
9	B—K3	B—K3
10	P—B3	....

DIAGRAM 57 Position after 10 P—B3

Black (FISCHER)

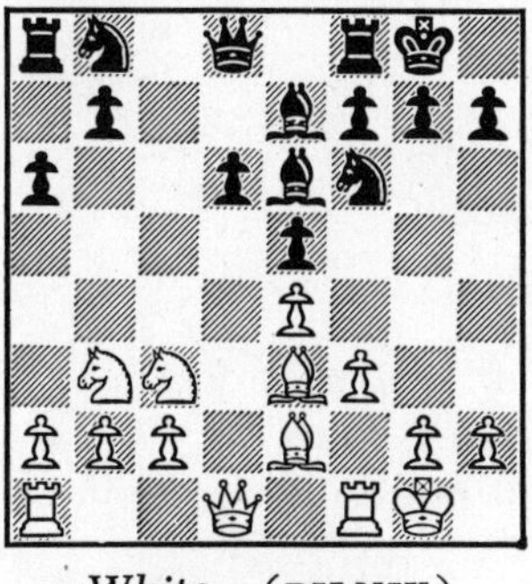

White (PILNIK)

White advances his King Bishop Pawn because he needs additional protection for his King Pawn in order to play N—Q5, a key move in this line. In addition, P—B3 enables his Queen to take up a station at the KB2 square later on.

10	....	Q—B2!?

Black can equalize with 10 . . . P—Q4, ridding himself of his backward Queen Pawn. However, this would lead to simplifying exchanges; hence he prefers a more complicated if cramped position. The same reasoning applies on the following move.

11	Q—K1	....

White forgoes the opportunity to play N—Q5 at an opportune moment.

11	....	QN—Q2
12	R—Q1	P—QN4

Black has counterplay in the half-open Queen Bishop file.

13	R—Q2	N—N3

Now White must always reckon with the strong counter . . . N—B5.

14	Q—B2	....

If now 14 . . . N—B5; 15 BxN, BxB; 16 KR—Q1 with marked pressure. Or 14 . . . N—B5; 15 BxN, PxB; 16 B—N6 followed by N—R5 with a strong game for White.

14	....	QR—N1!

Now Black threatens 15 . . . N—B5; 16 BxN, PxB winning a Pawn.

15	BxN	....

A reluctant but unavoidable decision, for after 15 N—R5 Black can free himself with 15 . . . P—Q4! as 16 BxN, RxB; 17 PxP?? will not do because of 17 . . . B—QB4! and Black wins.

15	....	RxB

Now Black has two Bishops against Bishop and Knight —a power in the endgame. In addition he is threatening to give up one of the Bishops to get a very strong position by 16 . . . BxN; 17 RPxB, P—Q4! (again menacing . . . B—B4!).

DIAGRAM 58 Position after 15 . . . RxB

Black (FISCHER)

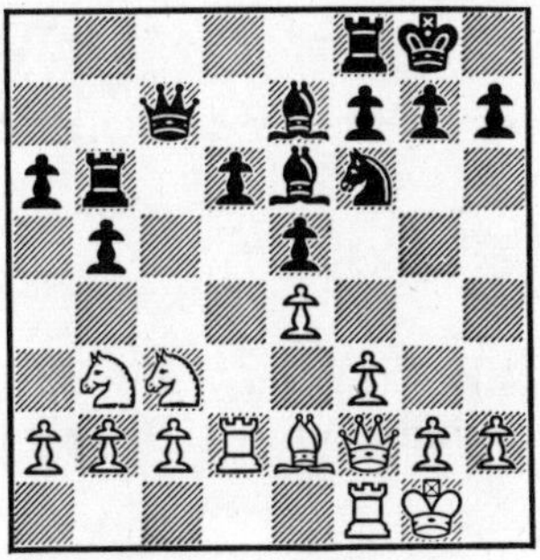

White (PILNIK)

16	N—Q5	NxN
17	PxN	B—Q2

White has banished the possibility of . . . P—Q4 but Black remains with a fine game. His immediate threat is . . . B—N4, winning a Pawn.

18	P—KB4	B—KB3!

Threatening to win a Pawn with . . . PxP. Black's King Bishop, originally his problem child, is now effectively posted.

19	P—B3	R/N3—N1

Black wants to play . . . P—QR4 and . . . P—N5 in order to open lines on the Queen-side and leave White with a weak Pawn because of the resulting exchanges.

20	PxP	BxP

The alternative 20 . . . PxP is tempting in order to prevent White from playing N—Q4. But after 20 . . . PxP; 21 P—Q6! White has a formidable passed Pawn.

21	N—Q4	P—N3
22	P—QR3	P—QR4!
23	K—R1	. . . .

With a view to the following endgame, it does not make good sense to withdraw the King to the side.

23	. . . .	P—N5!

This move is part of Black's over-all strategy. It also sets a deep trap.

24	BPxP	. . . .

Instead, 24 RPxP, PxP; 25 P—B4 was more solid, although it would reduce White's Bishop to a purely defensive status.

24	. . . .	PxP
25	R—B2	Q—N3
26	N—B6	. . . .

This is very attractive, as the double attack on Black's Rook and Queen Knight Pawn apparently leaves him with nothing better than 26 . . . BxN; 27 RxB, QxQ; 28 RxQ with a likely draw.

DIAGRAM 59 Position after 26 N—B6

Black (FISCHER)

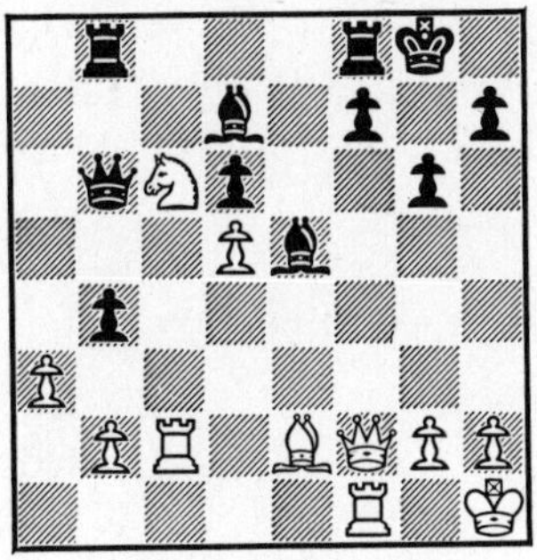

White (PILNIK)

26	....	PxP!!

Very fine. After 27 NxR, QxQ; 28 RxQ, P—R7!; 29 R—KB1, B—B4!; 30 R/R2—B1, BxNP; 31 R—R1 (not 31 N—B6, BxR; 32 RxB, B—N8 and the Pawn queens), BxR; 32 RxB, RxN White can resign, as 33 RxP allows Black to force mate.

27	QxQ	RxQ
28	PxP	R—R1!

Black fastens like a leech on the weak Pawn. White is in difficulties, for on 29 R—R2 Black wins the Pawn with 29 . . . R—N7! On the other hand, 29 R—KB3 will not do because of 29 . . . R—N8 ch; 30 B—B1, RxP! Now we see how well Black has succeeded with his strategy of opening lines on the Queen-side.

29	NxB	....

White removes the powerful Bishop and creates a counterchance in his passed Queen Pawn.

29	....	PxN
30	R—QB3	R—N7

Not an easy move to meet, as 31 R—K3 is refuted by 31 . . . RxB!; 32 RxR, B—N4; 33 R/R1—K1, BxR; 34 RxB, RxP and Black remains a Pawn ahead as his King Pawn is sacrosanct.

And if 31 B—B4, K—N2!; 32 P—Q6, P—B4; 33 B—Q5 (threatening BxR and also R—B7), Black has a powerful reply in 33 . . . R—R3! winning the Queen Pawn.

31	R—B7	B—B4

White struggles for counterplay.

32	P—N4	B—K5 ch
33	B—B3	B—Q6!

DIAGRAM 60 Position after 33 . . . B—Q6!

Black (FISCHER)

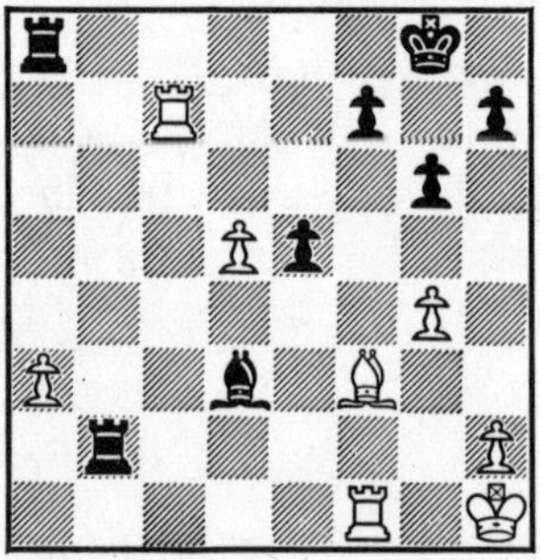

White (PILNIK)

White's best defense is 34 R—K1, P—K5!; 35 B—N2 (not 35 BxP?, R—K1 and wins; nor 35 P—Q6, PxB!; 36 P—Q7, P—B7!; 37 R—K8 ch, K—N2; 38 R—B1, R—Q1!! and wins, for if 39 RxR, B—K5 mate), P—B4 and Black will win in due course.

34	P—Q6?!	R—Q1
35	R—K1	RxQP
36	RxKP	. . . .

Suddenly the game looks drawish.

36	....	R—KB3!

White's menaced Bishop is trapped, as 37 B—N2 loses to 37 ... R—N8 ch while 37 B—Q5 permits 37 ... R—B8 mate.

37	R—K3	RxB!
38	RxR	B—K5
39	R/N7xP	R—KB7!
40	R—B8 ch	K—N2
	Resigns	

A superb ending.

38 *KING'S INDIAN DEFENSE*

ZURICH / 1959

This exciting game is a war of nerves. And, as we might confidently expect, the player with the stronger nerves wins the game.

	White	*Black*
	OLAFSSON	FISCHER
1	P—QB4	N—KB3
2	N—QB3	P—KN3
3	P—Q4	B—N2
4	P—K4	P—Q3
5	N—B3	Castles

This hard-boiled defense is a great favorite of Fischer's, for it is admirably suited to his style.

6	B—K2	P—K4
7	P—Q5	....

It is pointless to try to win a Pawn with 7 PxP, PxP; 8 QxQ, RxQ; 9 NxP because of 9 . . . NxP! and if 10 NxBP??, BxN ch, Black winning a piece.

7	....	QN—Q2
8	B—N5	....

An irritating pin which provokes Black to drive off the Bishop at the cost of weakening his King-side position with Pawn moves that create later targets for White's attack.

8	....	P—KR3
9	B—R4	P—R3

A versatile move. Black wants to move his King Knight in order to advance . . . P—KB4. But first he must unpin the Knight, which calls for . . . Q—K1, and this move in turn is prepared by . . . P—R3 which prevents White's N—QN5.

The combination of . . . P—R3 and . . . Q—K1 will also form a useful preparation for . . . P—QN4 later on, with valuable counterplay for Black.

DIAGRAM 61 Position after 9 . . . P—R3

Black (FISCHER)

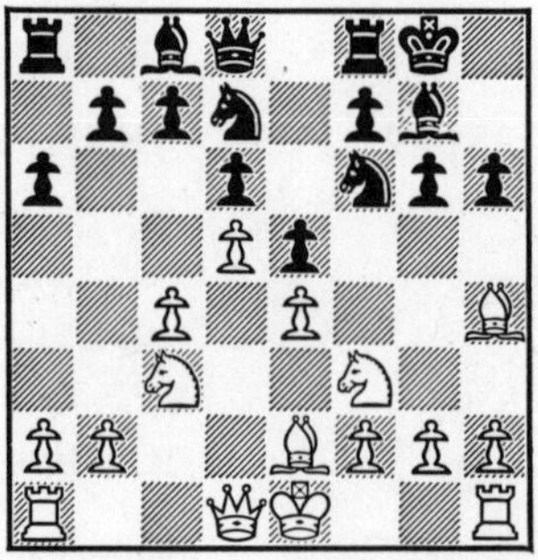

White (OLAFSSON)

10.	N—Q2	....

White also makes his preparations: he wants to be able to play P—B3 and P—KN4; these are moves directed against Black's eventual . . . P—KB4.

10	....	Q—K1
11	P—KN4	N—R2
12	Q—B2	....

White prepares to castle Queen-side, but 12 B—N3 followed by P—KR4 might be more germane here.

12	....	N—N4

With the interesting positional threat of . . . N—R6—B5.

13	P—KR3	N—B4

Provoking White to loosen up his position with P—N4. But White resists temptation.

14	Castles/Q	B—Q2
15	P—B3	N—R5
16	NxN	BxN
17	P—N3	B—Q2
18	B—B2	....

Again the Bishop is involved in a problem of timing. By playing 18 N—N1 White could have ruled out the reply 18 . . . P—QB4 because of 19 PxP *e.p.* winning a Pawn.

18	....	P—QB4!

Whereas if now 19 PxP *e.p.*, PxP; 20 N—N1, Black seizes the initiative with 20 . . . P—KB4! for if 21 KPxP, PxP; 22 RxP, PxP and Black recovers the Pawn with a very complicated game in prospect.

19	P—KR4	N—R2
20	B—K3	P—QN4

The logical continuation, but it turns out to have more defensive value (26 . . . R—R2!) than offensive potentialities.

21	N—N1	P—B4!?

Black's most aggressive continuation and also his riskiest.

22	NPxP	....

Naturally White captures in order to have attacking chances along the King Knight file.

22	....	KNPxP
23	KPxP!?	....

White likewise has the courage of his convictions. Since he is understandably reluctant to allow the position to be blockaded by . . . P—B5, he opens up the position despite the risks involved in unleashing Black's Bishops.

23	....	BxP
24	Q—Q2	....

Now Black can guard his menaced Pawn with 24 . . . R—B3, but this is too picayune for his taste. He prefers something far more sprightly.

DIAGRAM 62 Position after 24 Q—Q2

Black (FISCHER)

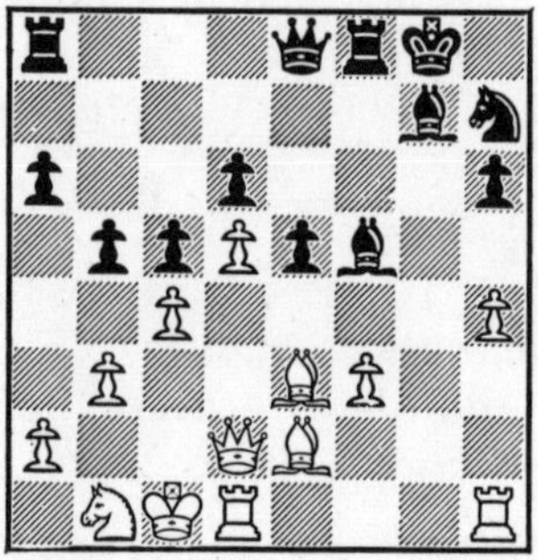

White (OLAFSSON)

24	....	P—K5!!?

A difficult move to answer, for example 25 PxKP (hoping for 25 . . . BxP?; 26 KR—N1, Q—K4; 27 RxB ch!), QxP!; 28 N—B3, Q—K4!; 29 N—N1, Q—R8; 30 B—Q3, BxB; 31 QxB, Q—N7 mate. Or 28 B—Q3, QxB/Q6; 29 QxQ, BxQ; 30 RxB, PxP; 31 PxP, QR—N1 and Black has a winning position.

Similarly, after 25 P—B4, Q—K2! followed by . . . Q—B3! Black's attack must succeed.

Finally, if 25 BxRP, KPxP; and White cannot play 26 BxP as 26 . . . BxN wins a piece.

25	QR—N1	KPxP
26	BxRP?	....

This loses. Best, according to Kmoch, is 26 RxB ch!, KxR; 27 BxP ch, K—R1; 28 BxR, QxB/B1; 29 Q—B3 ch, Q—B3; 30 QxQ ch, NxQ; 31 BxP, PxP; 32 PxP, B—Q6; 33 N—Q2, N—Q2; 34 P—R5, N—K4; 35 R—R4. Now Black can maintain strong pressure with 36 . . . R—KB1, with a distinct likelihood of regaining his Pawn with a superior position.

26	....	R—R2!

In the heat of the battle White has apparently failed to reckon with this fine resource.

27	BxB	RxB
28	RxR ch	....

Or 28 Q—R6, Q—K4! and Black's advanced King Bishop Pawn remains untouchable.

28	....	KxR

Now an interesting possibility is 29 Q—B3 ch, Q—K4; 30 QxP, BxN; 31 Q—N4 ch, B—N3; 32 P—R5, Q—R8 ch and Black wins.

29	B—Q3	PxP
30	R—N1 ch	K—R1

It no longer much matters what White does. For example, 31 PxP, BxB; 32 QxB, Q—K4 is decidedly in Black's favor.

31	Q—B3 ch	Q—K4
32	QxQ ch	....

Likewise after 32 BxB, RxB; 33 PxP, R—B5 Black must win.

32	....	PxQ
33	BxB	....

A quaint possibility here is 33 BxP, P—B7; 34 R—Q1, B—N5; 35 R—R1 (if 35 R—B1, B—R6 wins), B—B6; 36 R—R2 (or 36 R—B1, B—N7), BxP! and Black wins.

33	....	RxB
34	PxP	....

DIAGRAM 63 Position after 34 PxP

Black (FISCHER)

White (OLAFSSON)

The smoke of battle has cleared and Black's two connected passed Pawns must decide the issue in his favor.

34	....	N—B3
35	N—Q2	P—B7!
36	R—R1	....

After 36 R—B1 Black would win even more rapidly with 36 . . . P—K5.

36	. . . .	P—K5
37	K—Q1	. . . .

Or 37 N—B1, N—N5; 38 K—Q2, R—B6 and White is crippled.

37	. . . .	P—K6
38	N—B1	R—K4
39	K—K2	. . . .

If 39 N—N3, N—R4!; 40 N—K2, K—N2 and the inroad of Black's King is decisive.

39	. . . .	N—R4!

With the terrible threat of . . . N—B5 ch followed by . . . P—K7. White cannot maintain the blockade.

40	K—B3 Resigns	P—K7

The tranquil ending forms a fitting pendant to the stormy middle game.

39 *RUY LOPEZ*

ZURICH / 1959

The fact that the first twenty-one moves of this game are almost identical with those of Game 36 may come as a great surprise to the reader. But the explanation is simple enough: Fischer is certain that White's moves are the best, while Unzicker thinks that Black's play can be improved upon.

	White	*Black*
	FISCHER	UNZICKER
1	P—K4	P—K4
2	N—KB3	N—QB3
3	B—N5	P—QR3
4	B—R4	N—B3
5	Castles	B—K2
6	R—K1	P—QN4
7	B—N3	P—Q3
8	P—B3	Castles
9	P—KR3	N—QR4
10	B—B2	P—B4
11	P—Q4	Q—B2
12	QN—Q2	B—Q2
13	N—B1	KR—K1
14	N—K3	P—N3
15	PxKP	PxP
16	N—R2	QR—Q1
17	Q—B3	B—K3
18	N/R2—N4	NxN
19	PxN	....

DIAGRAM 64 Position after 19 PxN

Black (UNZICKER)

White (FISCHER)

Now the Tournament Book suggests the simplifying move 19 . . . N—B5, on the theory that if White avoids the exchange and plays 20 N—Q5 with the sequel 20 . . . BxN; 21 PxB White's resulting Queen Pawn will become rather insecure.

19	. . . .	Q—B3
20	P—N5	N—B5
21	N—N4	BxN
22	QxB	P—B3

Here Black branches off from Game 36, where Black played 22 . . . N—N3.

23	PxP	BxP

Black has opened up the second rank for full protection against a possible attack by White along the King Rook file. White therefore turns to the other wing.

24	P—R4!	N—N3

And not 24 . . . P—N5??; 25 B—N3 and wins.

25	PxP	PxP
26	B—K3	R—R1

Black means to dispute the file. The alternative 26 . . . N—B5 would be more than dubious in view of the reply 27 B—N3 creating a very serious weakness in Black's position.

27	KR—Q1	K—R1

Now Black is on the point of playing . . . N—B5 as the Knight can no longer be pinned. Hence White's next move, which cuts down the Knight's mobility appreciably.

28	P—QN3!	B—N2
29	Q—R4!	B—B3

The alternative 29 . . . RxR; 30 RxR, R—R1?; 31 RxR ch, NxR loses outright (32 Q—Q8 ch and mate follows).

30	B—N5	BxB
31	QxB	....

White's Queen is now unopposed in any invasion attempts on the black squares. Meanwhile Black's King Pawn and Bishop Pawn are under heavy pressure, the immediate threat being 32 RxR, NxR; 33 R—Q5, Q—B2; 34 Q—B6 ch, K—N1 and now White wins material with 35 P—QN4!! as Black must not play 35 . . . PxP because of 36 R—Q7!!, QxR; 37 B—N3 ch winning right off (Kmoch).

DIAGRAM 65 Position after 31 QxB

Black (UNZICKER)

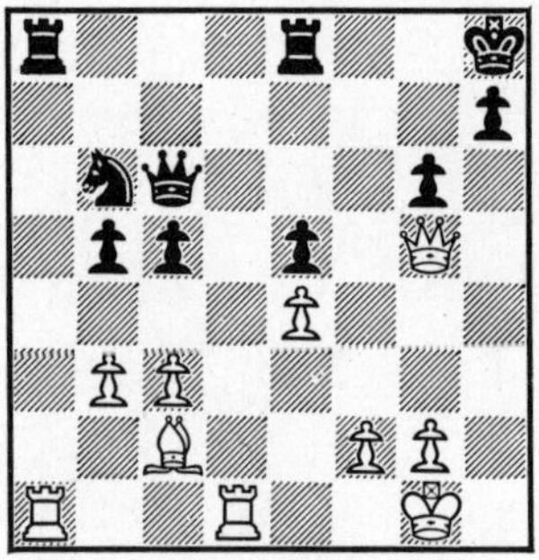

White (FISCHER)

Black cannot defend himself with 31 . . . N—Q2 in view of the continuation 32 RxR, RxR; 33 Q—K7!, R—R2; 34 RxN! and wins.

31	....	RxR
32	RxR	N—Q2

White can now continue promisingly with R—R7, but instead he finds a surprisingly powerful move.

33	B—Q1!	....

The idea is to bring this Bishop into effecive play. Thus, if 33 . . . QxP; 34 B—B3, Q—KB5; 35 QxQ, PxQ; 36 B—

B6!, R—Q1; 37 R—Q1 winning a piece—or 36 . . . R—K2; 37 R—R8 ch!, K—N2; 38 R—R7 with the same result, as 38 . . . R—K8 ch still leaves the Knight pinned.

33	....	N—B3

After 33 . . . Q—B3 White can continue effectively with 34 Q—K3 or Q—N4, with such moves as R—R7 and B—K2 kept in reserve.

34	R—R7!	Q—Q3

Not 34 . . . NxP?; 35 Q—R6 and White forces mate. And on 34 . . . N—N1 White strengthens the pressure with 35 Q—R4, P—R3; 36 B—K2 etc.

35	B—K2!	....

This quiet move reduces Black to desperation, as 35 . . . Q—B3 is simply answered by 36 BxP! Or 35 . . . R—QN1; 36 Q—R6, Q—B1; 37 QxQ ch, RxQ; 38 P—B3 and Black must lose material. Finally, if 35 . . . P—N5; 36 PxP, PxP; 37 R—KB7!, N—N1; 38 B—B4 and Black cannot hold out against the pressure.

35	....	R—K2

Black heads into an ending in which he hopes for drawing chances.

36	RxR	QxR
37	BxP	K—N2
38	B—K2	Q—QB2
39	Q—K3	....

White consolidates his position before trying to make more progress.

39	....	Q—R4
40	P—N3	Q—R6
41	K—N2!	....

White realizes that after 41 . . . QxP; 42 QxP he must win by advancing his Queen Bishop Pawn.

41	....	Q—R4
42	Q—Q3	Q—N3
43	Q—B4	Q—B3
44	B—Q3	Q—N3

DIAGRAM 66 Position after 44 . . . Q—N3

Black (UNZICKER)

White (FISCHER)

45	P—QN4!	....

Now White fashions a passed Pawn—an important step forward.

45	....	PxP
46	PxP	N—N5
47	Q—B5	QxQ

If Black evades the exchange of Queens, White advances his passed Pawn with rapidly decisive effect.

48	PxQ	K—B2
49	P—B4!	....

Now White gets a passed King Pawn.

49	....	K—K2

Black is willing to give up another Pawn as the Pawn on White's K4 square will hamper the mobility of White's Bishop. However, White gets around this difficulty by masterly maneuvers with his Bishop.

50	K—B3	N—B3
51	B—N5!	....

This rules out . . . N—Q2 as a reply to PxP.

51	....	K—K3
52	B—B4 ch	K—K2
53	P—B6!	....

Very fine: if Black plays 53 . . . K—Q3 then 54 PxP ch wins a piece (54 . . . KxKP; 55 P—B7).

53	....	N—K1
54	PxP	P—R3
55	K—K3	N—B2
56	K—Q4	P—R4

To stop the further progress of White's King, Black starts a diversion on the other wing to get a passed Pawn of his own. But White has the situation well in hand.

57	K—K3!	P—N4
58	B—K2!	P—R5

Against the alternative 58 . . . K—K3 White can proceed 59 K—Q4, P—R5 (after 59 . . . P—N5 Black is stopped on the King-side and his Pawns are vulnerable on the white squares); 60 PxP, PxP; 61 B—N4 ch with an easy win.

DIAGRAM 67 Position after 58 . . . P—R5

Black (UNZICKER)

White (FISCHER)

The rest is easy but the timing is enjoyable.

59	PxP	PxP
60	B—B4	N—K1
61	K—B4	K—Q1
62	K—N4	K—B2

Now 63 B—Q5 is certainly good enough, but White finds a neater line.

63	B—B7!	N—N2
64	KxP	KxP
65	K—N5	Resigns

For after 65 . . . K—Q2; 66 K—B6, N—K1 ch; 67 BxN ch, KxB; 68 K—K6 (or 68 P—K6) and White queens in a few moves. Another superb ending, and a most enjoyable one.

40 *SICILIAN DEFENSE*

CANDIDATES' TOURNAMENT / BLED / 1959

In this very exciting game Fischer takes the measure of one of the world's greatest players. The chances are that White's opening play was based on secret analysis and that Black's play was improvised. If so, Black's achievement is all the more creditable.

	White	*Black*
	KERES	FISCHER
1	P—K4	P—QB4
2	N—KB3	P—Q3
3	P—Q4	PxP
4	NxP	N—KB3
5	N—QB3	P—QR3
6	B—KN5	P—K3
7	P—B4	B—K2
8	Q—B3	Q—B2
9	Castles	QN—Q2
10	B—K2	....

While this developing move looks a lot more sedate than 10 P—KN4 (played in Game 43), it leads to even wilder play.

10	....	P—N4!?

Black dares his opponent to play P—K5.

DIAGRAM 68 Position after 10 . . . P—N4!?

Black (FISCHER)

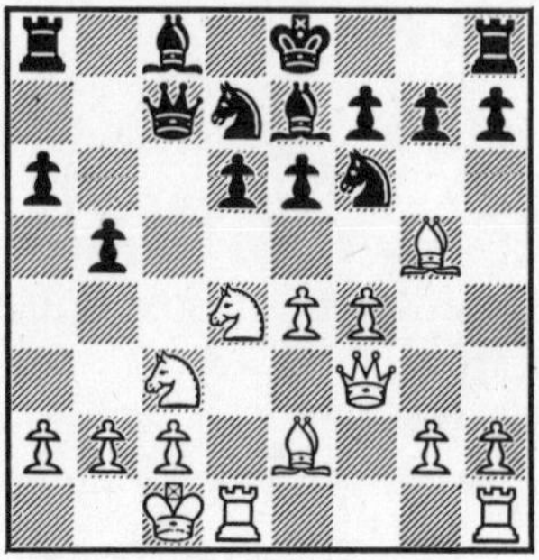

White (KERES)

The immediate 11 P—K5? will not do, for after 11 . . . B—N2; 12 PxN, BxQ; 13 BxB, PxP! White loses his Queen Bishop. Hence the following exchange.

11	BxN	NxB
12	P—K5!?	B—N2

White has reached the do-or-die stage, for after 13 Q—N3, PxP; 14 PxP, N—Q2; 15 QxP, QxP Black has a comfortable game.

13	PxN!?	BxQ
14	BxB	BxP!

Black seeks counterplay. After 14 . . . QR—B1; 15 PxB he would be decidedly on the defensive (if then 15 . . . QxP?; 16 N—B5! wins).

15	BxR	P—Q4!

The point: White's Bishop will not come out alive. And after 16 N/B3—K2 the sequel might be 16 . . . Castles; 17 B—B6, BxN; 18 NxB, QxP ch; 19 K—N1, Q—B2 threatening 20 . . . P—K4; 21 N—B5, P—N3! and Black wins a piece.

16	BxP	....

Now Black can easily go wrong, for example 16 . . . QxP ch?; 17 K—N1, BxN?; 18 B—B6 ch! followed by 19 N—K2! and White is ahead in material. And on 16 . . . QxP ch?; 17 K—N1, PxB White has a strong initiative with 18 NxQP.

16	....	BxN!
17	RxB	PxB
18	NxQP	Q—B4
19	R—K1 ch	K—B1

But not 19 . . . K—Q1?; 20 P—B3, K—B1; 21 P—KN4!, Q—R2; 22 R—K7 and White commands the board.

20	P—B3	....

DIAGRAM 69 Position after 20 P—B3

Black (FISCHER)

White (KERES)

With Rook, Knight, and Pawn for the Queen, White has roughly material equality. Once Black's Rook gets into play, the scales will surely tip in Black's favor. White must therefore make the most of the present phase.

20	....	P—KR4

Black hopes to get his Rook into the game by . . . R—R3.

21	P—B5	. . . .

Not the best. After 21 R—K5 (threatening 22 N—B6!) Black would still have a very difficult game on his hands. Euwe gives the following plausible sequence: 21 . . . Q—R2; 22 N—K7, P—N3; 23 P—B5!, K—N2; 24 PxP, PxP; 25 R—K6, R—KB1; 26 RxP ch, K—R2; 27 R/N6—Q6, R—B2; 28 N—Q5, P—R4; 29 N—B6 ch, K—N3 with unclear outcome.

21	. . . .	R—R3
22	P—B6	. . . .

To keep Black's Rook out of play.

22	. . . .	PxP
23	N—B4	. . . .

Euwe considers 23 N—K3 more solid: for example, 23 . . . R—N3; 24 R—Q5, Q—B1; 25 RxRP, Q—K3; 26 R-—Q5 etc.

23	. . . .	P—R5
24	R—Q8 ch	K—N2
25	R/K1—K8	. . . .

White threatens mate, but Black parries with no trouble.

25	. . . .	Q—N8 ch
26	K—Q2	Q—B7 ch
27	N—K2	R—N3

Ending White's threat.

28	P—KN3	P—B4
29	R—N8 ch	K—B3
30	RxR ch	PxR
31	PxP	QxP/R7
32	R—Q4	. . . .

White's last hope. He sets up a defense on the fourth rank to guard his King Rook Pawn and to prevent . . .

P—B5. But Black's delicate Queen maneuvers bring the desired result.

32	....	Q—R8

Black threatens to win material with . . . Q—QN8 or . . . Q—R8.

33	K—B2	K—K4

DIAGRAM 70 Position after 33 . . . K—K4

Black (FISCHER)

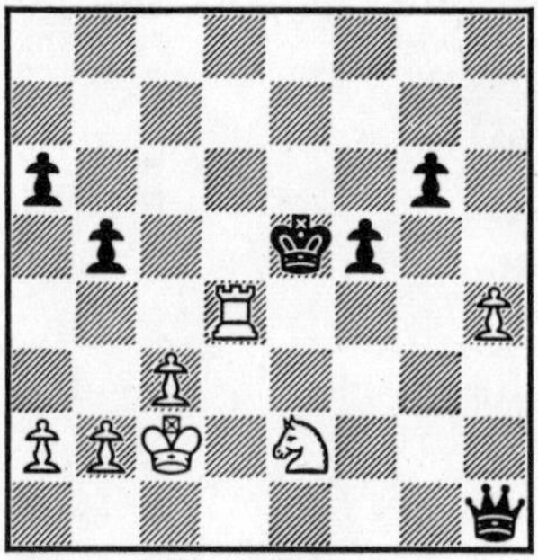

White (KERES)

White can only await the inevitable. A neat possibility pointed out by Kmoch is 34 R—QN4, Q—K8; 35 N—B4, Q—B7 ch; 36 K—Q3, QxN!; 37 RxQ, KxR; 38 P—N3, K—N6; 39 P—B4, PxP ch; 40 PxP, P—B5; 41 P—B5, P—B6; 42 P—B6, P—B7; 43 P—B7, P—B8/Q ch and wins.

34	P—R4	Q—KB8
35	N—B1	Q—N7 ch
36	K—N3	PxP ch
37	K—R3	....

Or 37 RxP, Q—KB7; 38 N—R2, P—B5 and the Pawn will queen.

37	....	Q—QB7
38	N—Q3 ch	K—B3
39	N—B5	Q—B8
40	RxP	Q—K6
41	NxP	....

Now the Knight is too far away to be of any use against the terrible King Bishop Pawn; but 41 RxP ch, K—N2 is equally hopeless for White.

41	....	P—B5
42	R—Q4	K—B4
43	N—N4	Q—K2

Just to make assurance doubly sure, Black picks up the Rook Pawn as well.

44	K—N3	QxP
45	N—Q3	P—N4
46	P—B4	Q—N6
47	P—B5	P—B6
48	K—B4	P—B7
49	NxP	QxN
50	P—B6	....

A forlorn hope.

50	....	QxP
51	K—B5	Q—B6 ch
52	K—Q5	P—N5
53	R—B4	....

Oversight or suicide? It doesn't matter.

53	....	Q—K4 mate

A memorable encounter.

41 *SICILIAN DEFENSE*

CANDIDATES' TOURNAMENT / BLED / 1959

This is a game which embodies the classic principle of attack on one wing with counterattack on the other. In such games timing is all. But whereas every move that White makes is timed to hit hard, Black does not function on the same high level. The early moves with the Queen have the predictable and unfortunate result that the Queen is out of touch with King-side defense and at the same time is exposed to tempo-gaining attack.

Had Black tried to make the best of the situation by finding the most economical and tenacious defense, he might still have managed to survive. His failure at this crucial level led to speedy disintegration.

	White	*Black*
	FISCHER	BENKO
1	P—K4	P—QB4
2	N—KB3	N—QB3
3	P—Q4	PxP
4	NxP	N—B3
5	N—QB3	P—Q3
6	B—QB4	Q—N3

One's first reaction is to distrust this move on the principle that such early Queen moves can generally be repulsed with gain of time.

In this case, however, the early Queen move takes on a certain attractiveness because the choice of a reply is rather puzzling. Thus, 7 N—N3 is safe enough, but it bunches White's pieces awkwardly on the Queen-side and virtually rules out the chances of a King-side attack. It is true that 7 N—B3 avoids this defect, but it blocks the advance of White's King Bishop Pawn, usually viewed as a basic component of a dashing King-side attack.

Still another alternative is 7 B—K3!?, but then Black

has 7 . . . QxP; 8 N/Q4—N5, Q—N5! (meeting White's primary threat of 9 QR—N1 which would win the Queen). In that case Black has no reason to fear 10 N—B7 ch, K—Q1; 11 NxR ch followed by 12 . . . QxB/B5.

DIAGRAM 71 Position after 6 . . . Q—N3

Black (BENKO)

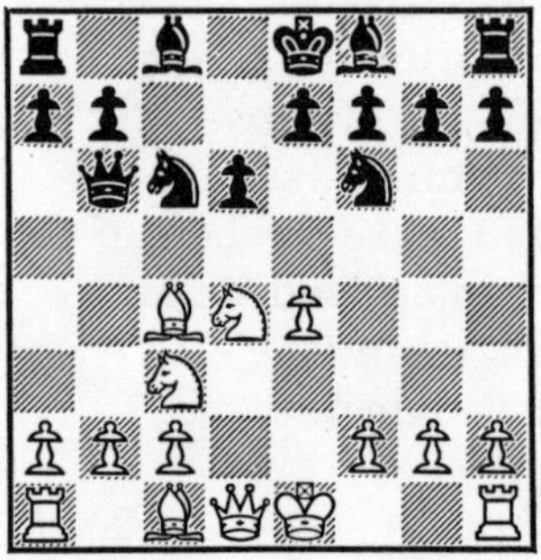

White (FISCHER)

7	KN—K2	. . . .

In the light of the previous comments, this discreet withdrawal makes good sense. Meanwhile White leaves the path open for the future advance of his King Bishop Pawn.

7	. . . .	P—K3
8	Castles	B—K2
9	B—N3	. . . .

White rules out the loss of his Queen Knight Pawn before developing the other Bishop.

9	. . . .	Castles
10	K—R1	. . . .

The necessary preliminary to advancing his King Bishop Pawn.

10	. . . .	N—QR4

As we shall see, it is dangerous for Black to remove a piece bearing on the center. Here or next move it would have been a sound idea to play . . . B—Q2 or perhaps . . . R—Q1 first.

11	B—N5	Q—B4
12	P—B4	P—N4?!

Black is playing with fire. This move initiates a daring plan which forces an immediate crisis.

13	N—N3	. . . .

White guards his King Pawn against . . . P—N5. He also threatens 14 P—K5!, PxP; 15 BxN, BxB; 16 QN—K4, Q—K2; 17 N—R5 (intending 18 N/K4xB ch, PxN; 19 Q—N4 ch and mate next move).

13	. . . .	P—N5

If White "sensibly" retreats his attacked Knight by 14 N/B3—K2, Black replies 14 . . . B—R3 with a good game. So White is practically forced to play:

14	P—K5!	. . . .

Now Black realizes that the intended 14 . . . PxN can be answered by 15 PxN, BxP; 16 BxB, PxB; 17 Q—N4 ch, K—R1; 18 Q—R4! and White has a winning attack.

14	. . . .	PxP
15	BxN	. . . .

DIAGRAM 72 Position after 15 BxN

Black (BENKO)

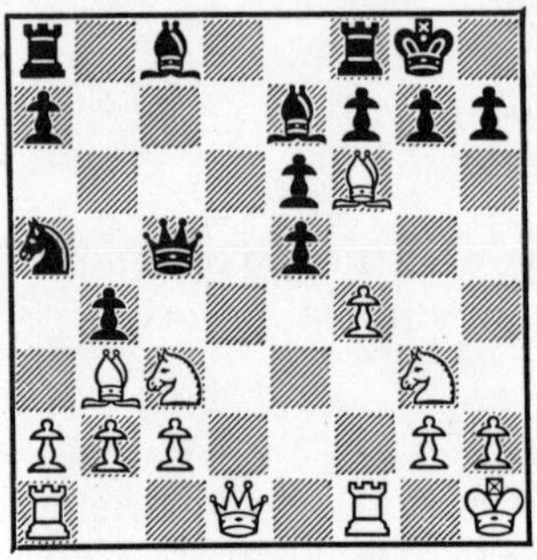

White (FISCHER)

15	....	PxB?

This loses, as does 15 . . . BxB; 16 QN—K4 etc.

According to Kmoch, the best line is 15 . . . PxN!; 16 N—K4, Q—N5. Then if 17 Q—N4, BxB; 18 NxB ch, K—R1; 19 Q—R4, P—KR3!; 20 N—N4, PxP and Black can hold the position.

16	N/B3—K4!	Q—Q5

Black hopes to guard against the subsequent mating threats at his KB3 and KN2 squares. This proves to be a forlorn hope.

17	Q—R5!	....

Black's broken-up King-side is an inviting target, the main threat being Q—R6 followed by N—R5.

If Black plays 17 . . . P—B4 there follows 18 KR—Q1!, QxP; 19 QR—N1!, Q—R6; 20 Q—R6! (threatens N—R5), P—B3; 21 N—R5, R—B2; 22 N/R5xP ch, K—R1 (if 22 . . . BxN; 23 NxB ch, RxN; 24 R—Q8 ch forcing mate); 23 N—N5, R—N2; 24 N/N5xRP and wins.

17	....	NxB
18	Q—R6!	....

Threatening to force mate with 19 N—R5 etc.

18	....	PxP
19	N—R5	P—B4
20	QR—Q1!	....

Even stronger than 20 N/K4—B6 ch, BxN; 21 NxB ch, QxN; 22 QxQ, NxR; 23 RxN. As played, White wins more material.

20	....	Q—K4

The alternative 20 . . . QxP? would be altogether disastrous because of 21 P—B3! shutting out the Black Queen.

21	N/K4—B6 ch	BxN
22	NxB ch	QxN
23	QxQ	N—B4
24	Q—N5 ch!	....

This leads to the winning of more material.

24	....	K—R1
25	Q—K7	B—R3

Or 25 . . . N—Q2; 26 RxN etc.

26	QxN	BxR
27	RxB	Resigns

A very difficult and exciting game.

42 *SICILIAN DEFENSE*

CANDIDATES' TOURNAMENT / BLED / 1959

In this game Fischer displays the attributes of a grandmaster: his play is sharp, bold, logical. The most significant feature of all is that Gligoric, one of the world's greatest players, is made to look like a tyro.

	White	*Black*
	FISCHER	GLIGORIC
1	P—K4	P—QB4
2	N—KB3	N—QB3
3	P—Q4	PxP
4	NxP	N—KB3
5	N—QB3	P—Q3
6	B—QB4	....

Fischer's trademark.

6	....	B—Q2
7	B—N3	....

Not essential, but it establishes the Bishop in a secure position.

7	....	P—KN3
8	P—B3	N—QR4

Played not so much with the idea of continuing . . . NxB as with the intention of enforcing . . . N—B5 after occupying the Queen Bishop file.

9	B—N5	B—N2
10	Q—Q2	P—KR3

This is of doubtful utility as it weakens the King-side. However, after 10 . . . Castles, White could force a favorable exchange of Bishops with 11 B—R6.

11	B—K3	QR—B1
12	Castles/Q	N—B5

DIAGRAM 73 Position after 12 . . . N—B5

Black (GLIGORIC)

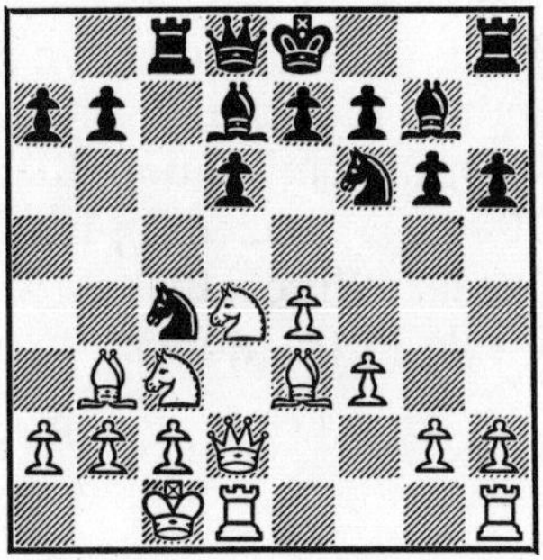

White (FISCHER)

13 Q—K2! . . . .

This quiet move is probably the finest in the whole game. Most players would automatically choose 13 BxN on the theory that White's black-square Bishop is his more important Bishop.

Fischer, however, sees more deeply into the position. White's Bishop on QN3 has a terrific diagonal which will become even more important when White finally begins his direct assault on the Black King. In addition, the King Bishop contributes substantially to the defense of White's King.

13 . . . . NxB

Falling in with White's plans, because the Knight cannot be maintained at his outpost (if 13 . . . Q—B2?; 14 N/Q4—N5 is disastrous for Black).

14 QxN Castles

Black's King cannot remain in the center indefinitely, for White is threatening a punishing advance in the center with P—B4 and P—K5.

15 P—N4 . . . .

Beginning the indicated Pawn-storming attack which involves several predictable considerations. By continuing with P—KR4 and P—N5 White will force open a file for direct King-side attack.

Secondly, by driving off the protective Knight, he will be in a position to play the powerful N—Q5.

To prevent this brutal occupation Black will feel compelled to play . . . P—K3, weakening his Queen Pawn.

And, as we shall see, White's Bishop will play an important if unobtrusive role in the attack.

15	....	Q—R4
16	P—KR4	P—K3

This protects his Queen 4 square and breaks the diagonal of White's Bishop, but it cannot hold the fort. However, there is no promising alternative.

17	N/Q4—K2	R—B3
18	P—N5	PxP
19	PxP	N—R4

With the futile hope of blocking the King Rook file; but there is always the latent threat of RxN at a propitious moment.

20	P—B4	KR—B1

An empty demonstration. White's position is much too solid to be in any danger.

21	K—N1	Q—N3
22	Q—B3	....

Now P—B5 looms up as a menacing possibility. White threatens 23 P—B5, KPxP; 24 PxP, BxP; 25 RxN and wins.

22	....	R—B4

This rules out the variation just shown, but by no means does it solve Black's troubles.

DIAGRAM 74 Position after 22 . . . R—B4

Black (GLIGORIC)

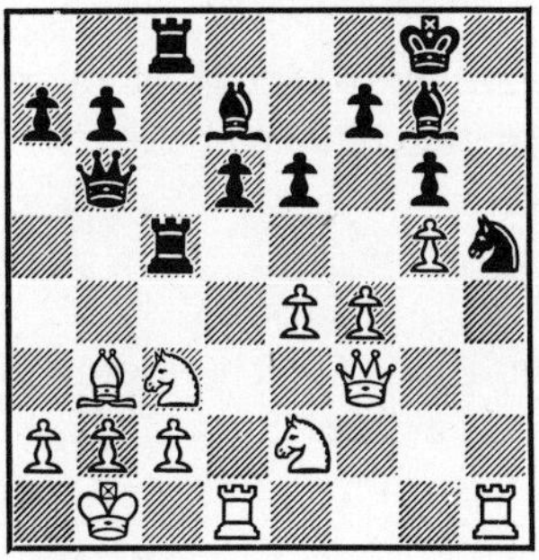

White (FISCHER)

23 Q—Q3! . . . .

A powerful, subtle, and well-timed move. Obviously Black cannot defend the weak Pawn with 23 . . . R/B1—B3? for then 24 N—R4 wins the exchange.

Nor, as Kmoch points out, would 23 . . . R/B4—B3 do: 24 P—B5!, KPxP; 25 RxN, PxP; 26 NxP, PxR; 27 N—B6 ch, BxN; 28 Q—N6 ch! (White's Bishop comes to life) and White has a quick mate.

And on 23 . . . B—B1 White keeps his threats intact with 24 QR—B1 or 24 R—R4 etc.

23 . . . . BxN?

Succumbing to a devilish positional trap.

24 NxB NxP

Black has been allowed to win a Pawn but the price is a heavy one: opening of the King Bishop file for White's forces.

25 Q—B3 N—R4

After 25 . . . P—K4 the White Bishop's diagonal has been opened as well. White can then continue forcefully with 26 N—Q5 or 26 N—K2.

26	RxN!	. . . .

At last this sacrifice, which has been simmering since 19 . . . N—R4, can take place.

26	. . . .	PxR
27	QxP	. . . .

Not one of the Black pieces defends the unfortunate King. Nor is flight feasible: 27 . . . K—B1; 28 Q—R8 ch, K—K2; 29 Q—B6 ch, then 30 R—R1 and mate follows.

27	. . . .	B—K1

This provides for the flight of Black's King by . . . K—B1 —K2—Q2. Hence White's fine reply, which nails the King down.

28	Q—R6!	RxN

Not that it matters.

29	PxR	RxP

Or 29 . . . Q—K6; 30 R—R1, QxBP; 31 P—N6, Q—N2; 32 Q—R2! and Black is amazingly helpless.

30	P—N6!	. . . .

Threatening to win with 31 P—N7.

30	. . . .	PxP
31	R—R1	Q—Q5
32	Q—R7 ch	Resigns

For after 32 . . . K—B1; 33 R—KB1 ch forced mate.

43 SICILIAN DEFENSE

CANDIDATES' TOURNAMENT / BLED / 1959

Defeating a former World Champion in the last round made a very fitting conclusion to this tournament for Fischer. A great achievement, and a portent of things to come.

	White	*Black*
	SMYSLOV	FISCHER
1	P—K4	P—QB4
2	N—KB3	P—Q3
3	P—Q4	PxP
4	NxP	N—KB3
5	N—QB3	P—QR3
6	B—KN5	....

Having the freer position, White plans a general advance of his King-side Pawns. The expanded development of the Bishop avoids its being locked in after P—B4; and on KN5 the Bishop exerts a certain amount of pressure on Black's game.

6	....	P—K3
7	P—B4	B—K2
8	Q—B3	....

White's opening plan calls for early development of his Queen in order to make room for Queen-side castling. However, the more plausible 8 Q—Q3 exposes the Queen to later attack by . . . QN—Q2—B4; while on 8 Q—Q2, P—R3 White must exchange (9 B—R4?, NxP!).

8	....	Q—B2
9	Castles	QN—Q2
10	P—KN4	....

Here we branch off from Game 40 against Keres, who played 10 B—K2. The actual move has pros and cons. It presages an aggressive King-side policy; and on the other hand, it involves a certain looseness on the long diagonal which has damaging implications for White.

10	....	P—N4

DIAGRAM 75 Position after 10 . . . P—N4

Black (FISCHER)

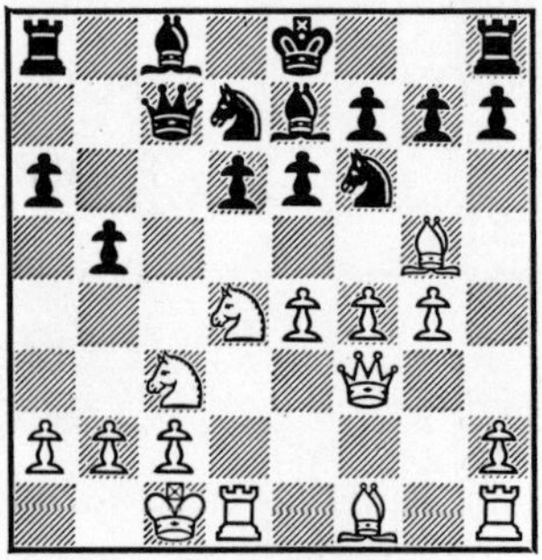

White (SMYSLOV)

11	BxN	NxB

In his game with Gligoric at Zurich earlier in the year Fischer continued 11 . . . PxB; 12 B—N2, B—N2; 13 KR—K1, Castles/Q; 14 P—QR3, N—N3; 15 R—Q3, K—N1; 16 KR—Q1 with a very comfortable position for White.

12	P—N5	N—Q2
13	B—R3	....

Not the most exact. The right move is 13 P—QR3! as in an earlier Gligoric-Fischer game from the same tournament, which continued 13 . . . B—N2; 14 B—R3, Castles/Q; 15 P—B5!, BxP ch; 16 K—N1, P—K4? (a mistake in an already bad position); 17 N/Q4xP! and White has a winning position.

13	....	P—N5!

By dislodging the Knight Black creates a potential threat against White's King Pawn and makes . . . P—Q4 feasible. He is also protecting himself against the possible sacrifice BxP etc.—though this latter point is destined to remain in the nebulous stage.

14	N/B3—K2	B—N2

Now 15 BxP fails because of 15 . . . PxB; 16 NxP, Q—B5!; 17 NxP ch, K—B2 and Black has too many threats.

15	K—N1	N—B4
16	N—KN3	....

The jumbled position of White's forces on the King-side does not augur well for his prospects.

16	....	P—Q4!

The reply 17 PxP? is ruled out because of 17 . . . BxQP winning the exchange. And, since the alternative 17 P—N5 looks unpromising, Smyslov decides on an enterprising if inconclusive Pawn offer which is partly based on the reasonable hope of confusing the opponent. However, Black's cold-blooded response leaves little hope for White.

17	P—B5?!	QPxP
18	Q—N4	KPxP!

Although 18 . . . P—K4 looks safer, it leaves White with good prospects of recovering his Pawn after 19 N—N3 etc.

19	N/Q4xP	P—N3!
20	NxB	QxN

DIAGRAM 76 Position after 20 . . . QxN

Black (FISCHER)

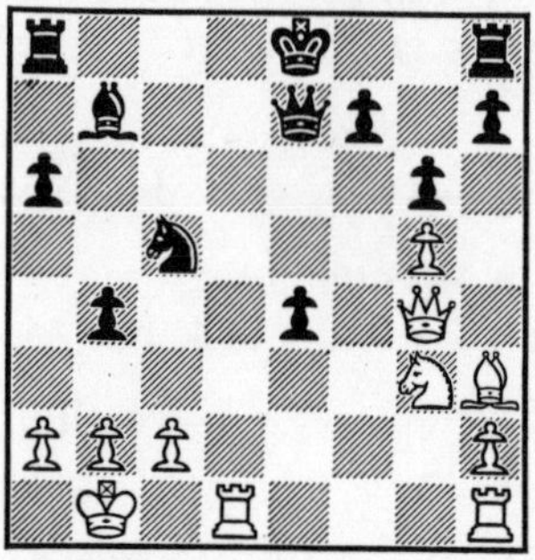

White (SMYSLOV)

Though Black's King Pawn looks anemic, Black has ample defensive resources. And since this is a passed Pawn, it has the potential of becoming very powerful later on.

Black has an interesting threat here: 21 . . . P—R3! winning another Pawn, for if 22 PxP?, B—B1! and White loses a piece.

If White avoids this and tries to win the King Pawn, the following line is an interesting possibility: 21 B—N2, Castles; 22 KR—K1, KR—K1; 23 R—Q4?, N—K3! and as Kmoch points out, 24 NxP is refuted by 24 . . . NxR!; 25 N—B6 ch, QxN! etc.

21	Q—B4	Castles
22	R—Q6	QR—Q1
23	R—KB6	R—Q4
24	B—N4	N—Q2!

White is trying very hard to create complications, but Black is just as inventive. He does not fear 25 NxP? for then 25 . . . R—Q5 wins a piece.

25	R—KB1	. . . .

Can White really be hoping for 25 . . . NxR??; 26 PxN when White is attacking the Queen and threatening 27 Q—R6 as well?

25	. . . .	P—K6!
26	P—N3	. . . .

To avoid any mating possibilities on the back rank.

26	. . . .	R—Q7!

Counterattack. Black threatens 27 . . . NxR!; 28 PxN, Q—B4; 29 R—B1, P—N4 or 29 B—B5, KR—Q1; 30 Q—R6?, R—Q8 ch forcing mate.

27	BxN	RxB
28	R—K1	R—K1
29	P—KR4	Q—B4!

DIAGRAM 77 Position after 29 . . . Q—B4!

Black (FISCHER)

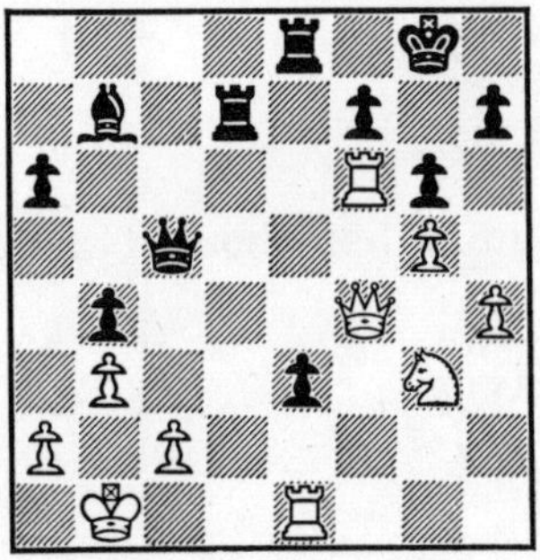

White (SMYSLOV)

Black is quite safe and has now seized the initiative. He is on the point of playing . . . Q—B6 or . . . R—Q7 or . . . R—Q5—all strong moves. White therefore sees himself forced to offer the exchange of Queens, even at the cost of another Pawn.

30	Q—B4	QxQ
31	PxQ	R—Q5

A plausible possibility here is 32 R—N6, B—B6!; 33 RxNP, R—Q8 ch!; 34 RxR, BxR and Black wins a piece with 35 . . . P—K7.

32	P—B5	. . . .

White's last hope: the passed Pawn affords him some counterplay.

32	. . . .	RxP
33	P—B6	B—B1
34	R—Q6	R—QB5
35	K—N2	K—N2
36	K—N3	R—N5
37	N—K2	R—K3!

. . . RxP looks good enough, but Black is determined to liquidate the troublesome passed Pawn.

38	R/K1—Q1	R—N7
39	N—B4	RxR
40	RxR	R—Q7!
41	R—Q3	R—B7

Black's sharp timing hereabouts is notable.

42	R—Q4	P—K7
43	N—Q3	B—B4
44	P—B7	R—B6!

Threatening . . . P—K8/Q or . . . RxN ch and thereby forcing some wholesale bloodletting.

45	P—B8/Q	BxQ
46	R—K4	B—B4
47	RxKP	BxN
48	PxB	RxP ch
49	KxP	R—Q4
50	R—KN2	P—R3!

This leaves Black with two connected passed Pawns.

51	PxP ch	KxP
52	P—R4	P—N4
53	R—QB2	R—Q3
54	K—B5	R—K3
	Resigns	

The passed Pawns win easily. Black's poise is really phenomenal for a sixteen-year-old youngster.

44 *QUEEN'S GAMBIT DECLINED*

UNITED STATES CHAMPIONSHIP (ROSENWALD TOURNAMENT) / 1959–60

In recent years the chess world has experienced such an increase in the number of first-class players that it has become more and more difficult to achieve a clear-cut advantage. Thanks to this state of affairs, technique has become more and more applicable to all but invisible advantages. Fischer is a past master of this modern art of "making something out of nothing."

	White	*Black*
	DENKER	FISCHER
1	P—Q4	N—KB3
2	P—QB4	P—K3
3	N—KB3	P—Q4
4	N—B3	B—N5
5	B—N5	. . . .

Despite its aggressive appearance, this move is not particularly promising. Possibly 5 P—K3 followed by 6 P—QR3 offers more.

5	. . . .	P—KR3

This practically forces the following exchange, unless White wants to undertake a rather dubious gambit with 6 B—R4, PxP; 7 P—K3 (if 7 P—K4, P—KN4! Or: 7 Q—R4 ch, N—B3; 8 P—K3, B—Q2!; 9 BxP?, NxP! etc.), P—QN4 etc.

6	BxN	QxB
7	PxP	....

Here too is a move without sting, freeing Black's Queen Bishop for an easy development. Simply 7 P—K3 is in order.

7	....	PxP
8	R—B1	Castles
9	P—QR3	BxN ch
10	RxB	P—B3
11	P—K3	P—QR4!

White's usual policy in positions of this sort is to play P—QN4—5 in the hope of weakening Black's position on the Queen-side. But now this maneuver becomes doubtful: for example, 12 P—QN4, PxP; 13 PxP, Q—K2! etc.

12	B—Q3	....

Having played a passive opening, White belatedly turns aggressive. Here 12 B—K2 is more in the spirit of the play up to this point.

12	....	B—N5

Whenever Black can safely play this move—a rare occurrence—we may be sure that he has survived the rigors of the opening stage.

13	P—R3	B—R4
14	P—KN4	....

Since White's attacking chances are virtually nil, this move merely signifies a weakening of his position.

14	....	B—N3
15	N—K5	BxB
16	QxB	Q—K2

Getting ready to develop his Knight at last.

17	Q—B5	....

To prevent . . . N—Q2; but Black carries out his idea effortlessly.

17	....	R—Q1
18	R—N1	....

White is still thining in terms of attack. It will be interesting to see how Black squelches this idea.

18	....	N—Q2
19	NxN	RxN
20	P—N5	R—Q3!

An admirable move which consolidates Black's defense. White should now continue 21 P—N6 courting 21 . . . PxP; 22 RxNP, RxR; 23 QxR. Instead, he continues the "attack." That way lies disaster.

21	P—KR4?	....

Thanks to Black's masterly play, this Pawn is immediately stamped as a weakness.

DIAGRAM 78 Position after 21 P—KR4?

Black (FISCHER)

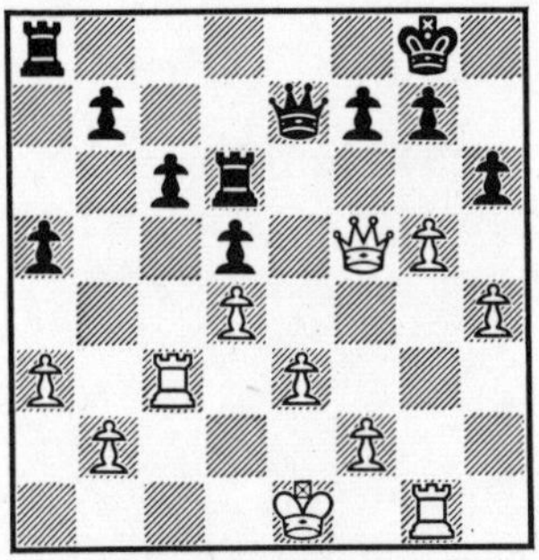

White (DENKER)

21	....	P—KR4!

This closes the King Knight file once for all and in addition fixes White's King Rook Pawn as a weakness. This latter point is instructively illustrated in the variation 22 P—N6, PxP; 23 RxNP, RxR; 24 QxR, QxKRP and Black is a Pawn to the good.

22	K—K2	....

With the castling privilege gone, White has to be thinking about getting his King into safety. The actual move is a loss of time, as will be seen on move 23, but it is questionable whether K—Q2 is better, for it leads White's King into the zone where he has most to fear—the Queen-side. The reason for this is that Black had had his eye for a long time on the possibility . . . P—QN3 followed by . . . P—B4. Once this advance comes off, lines will be opened, and if White's King is in the neighborhood, the consequences will be very unhealthy.

22	....	P—KN3!
23	Q—B3	R—K3

See the previous note. Black threatens 24 . . . R—K5 with a view to 25 . . . RxQP or 25 . . . RxRP.

24	K—Q2	R—K5
25	Q—R3	Q—B2

Preparing for . . . P—N3. White parries, but he cannot permanently restrain Black's project.

26	R/N1—QB1	QR—K1!

With a view to . . . R—N5 followed by . . . QR—K5. This threat provokes a new weakness in White's Pawn position.

DIAGRAM 79 Position after 26 . . . QR—K1

Black (FISCHER)

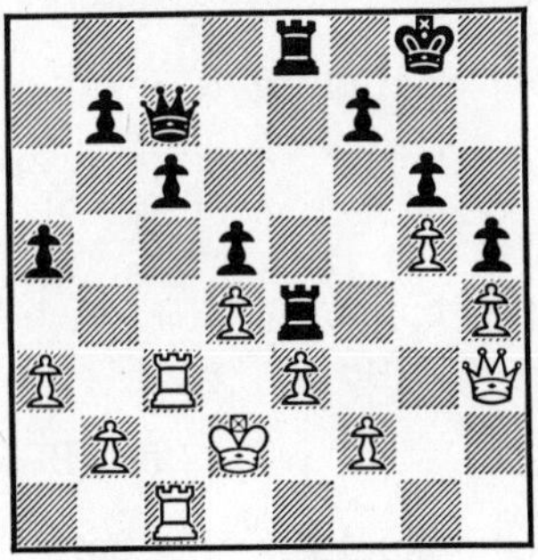

White (DENKER)

27	P—B3	R/K5—K3

Now that Black has protected his Queen Bishop Pawn a third time, he is ready for . . . P—N3.

If White tries 28 P—N4 (to hinder the eventual . . . P—QB4) he merely succeeds in overextending himself still further: 28 P—N4, PxP; 29 PxP, Q—K2 and Black wins a Pawn.

28	R—K1	P—N3!

At last.

29	K—B2	P—QB4!
30	PxP	. . . .

There is no good move. If, for example, 30 K—N1 Black can continue 30 . . . P—B5 followed by . . . P—N4—5. An excellent alternative is 30 . . . Q—Q3! which unpins Black's Queen Bishop Pawn, heightening his breakthrough possibilities.

30	. . . .	P—Q5!

The demolition proceeds with heartwarming energy.

31	BPxP	QxP
32	R—Q3	. . . .

In reply to 32 R—N3 Black plays a Rook check which wins a Rook.

32	....	R—N1!

Each Black move at this point is bone-crushing.

33	P—N3	R—QB3 ch
34	K—N2	....

On 34 K—Q2 Black has an attractive win with 34 . . . Q—B4!; 35 K—K2, Q—B7 ch; 36 R—Q2, P—Q6 ch etc.

34	....	R—B6!

Apparently Black visualizes the homeless White King's demise on the sixth rank.

DIAGRAM 80 Position after 34 . . . R—B6!

Black (FISCHER)

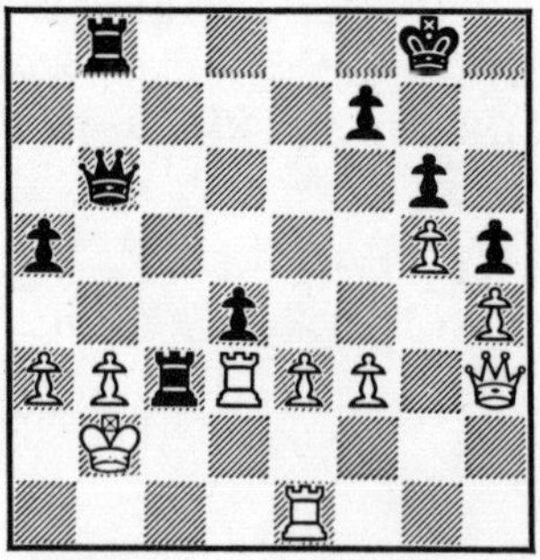

White (DENKER)

35	RxR	PxR ch
36	KxP	QxNP ch
37	K—Q2	Q—R7 ch!
38	K—Q3	R—Q1 ch
39	K—K4	Q—B5 ch
40	K—K5	R—Q4 ch
	Resigns	

After 41 K—B6 Black forces a quick mate with 41 . . . Q—B3 ch etc., or 41 . . . Q—B6 ch. A very rewarding game, Black's graceful handling of the heavy pieces being particularly noteworthy.

45 *KING'S INDIAN DEFENSE*

INTERNATIONAL TEAM TOURNAMENT / LEIPZIG / 1960

When a player makes as many mistakes as White does in this game, we are apt to forget the role played by his opponent. It is only fair to point out, therefore, that Black's admirably steady play fully exploits White's sins of omission and commission.

	White	*Black*
	SZABO	FISCHER
1	P—Q4	N—KB3
2	P—QB4	P—KN3
3	N—QB3	B—N2
4	P—K4	Castles
5	B—N5	P—Q3
6	Q—Q2	P—B4!

This thrust at White's center is intended to enhance the power of the fianchettoed Bishop along the long diagonal.

7	P—Q5	P—K3

Still trying to undermine White's center.

8	B—Q3	. . . .

There is nothing very pressing about this developing move. Instead, castling would give White a very promising position.

8	. . . .	PxP

If White replies 9 BPxP he remains with a broad and imposing-looking center, but he cedes Black a Queen-side majority of Pawns.

9	NxP	....

This looks more formidable than it actually is, as White's hope of exploiting the pin is illusory.

9	....	B—K3!

Black wants to get rid of the annoying Knight at the first opportunity.

DIAGRAM 81 Position after 9 . . . B—K3!

Black (FISCHER)

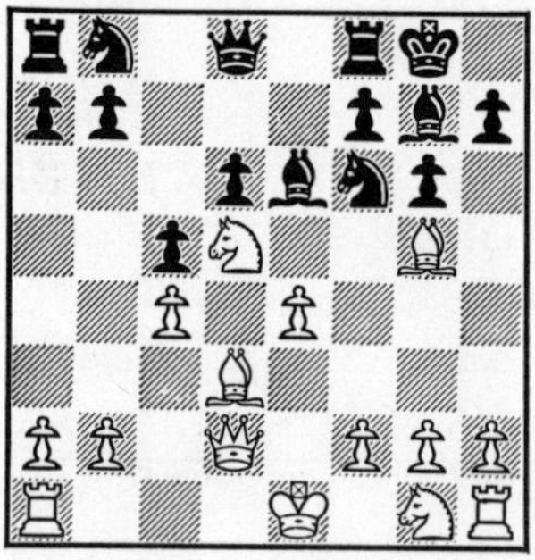

White (SZABO)

10	N—K2	....

This move is not calculated to give Black any trouble. Nor is the alternative 10 NxN ch, BxN; 11 BxB, QxB; 12 N—K2 particularly impressive, for the White Bishop is hemmed in by its own Pawns, and the weakness of Black's backward Queen Pawn seems quite bearable.

10	....	BxN

Black lightens the pressure on his game and closes the Queen file so that the backwardness of his Queen Pawn no longer matters.

11	KPxB	QN—Q2
12	Castles/K	N—K4
13	P—B4?	. . . .

This superficial move leads to trouble, as it weakens White's K3 square. White seems to have no inkling of the coming struggle for control of the King file. In this context the colorless N—B3 followed by KR—K1 was much safer.

13	. . . .	NxB
14	QxN	P—KR3
15	B—R4	R—K1
16	QR—K1	Q—N3!

Black gets out of the pin and attacks White's Queen Knight Pawn. This proves more troublesome than White has anticipated—if he really has anticipated it.

17	BxN?	. . . .

A positional blunder of the first magnitude. White pits a short-stepping Knight against a long-range Bishop—a hopeless undertaking.

In addition, as we shall see, White's Bishop was needed to provide additional protection for White's Rook at K1.

The right way, then, was 17 P—QN3 and if 17 . . . N—N5; 18 N—B3 and White has reasonable defensive prospects.

17	. . . .	BxB
18	P—B5	. . . .

This deprives White of his command of the K5 square, but by this time it no longer matters.

18	. . . .	P—N4!

DIAGRAM 82 Position after 18 . . . P—N4!

Black (FISCHER)

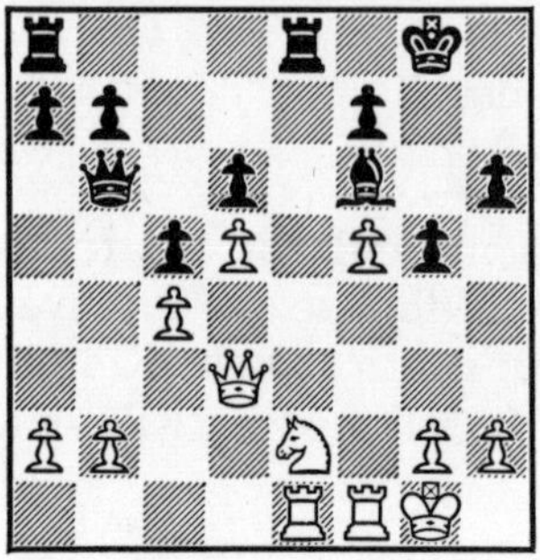

White (SZABO)

Now White must guard his Queen Knight Pawn. On 19 R—N1 Black doubles Rooks on the King file and maintains control of the file; an important strategic advantage.

White therefore tries a different way and gets into even more trouble.

19	P—QN3	Q—R4!

Very strong. Black attacks the Queen Rook Pawn and at the same time creates a pin on the Knight along the King file.

For example, after 20 P—QR4, B—Q5 ch!; 21 K—R1, R—K6 followed by 22 . . . QR—K1 Black has a clearly won game.

By the same token, after 20 Q—N1, R—K6; 21 N—N3, QR—K1; 22 RxR, RxR Black has a strategically won game.

20	R—B1	. . . .

But this is sheer collapse.

20	. . . .	QxP
21	R—B2	R—K6!

Neat simplification. White has little choice, for after 22 RxQ, RxQ Black has an easy win.

22	QxR	QxR
23	K—R1	P—QR4!
24	P—R4	P—R5
	Resigns	

White's capitulation is sudden but not unjustified, because he must lose still another Pawn in a situation where Black has all the play (25 PxP, QxQBP etc.). Fischer has shown his capabilities in this curious game.

46 *KING'S INDIAN DEFENSE*

INTERNATIONAL TEAM TOURNAMENT / LEIPZIG / 1960

Most masters start their careers with an enterprising style that gradually hardens into conservatism. In Fischer's play we have seen the reverse tendency. Growing maturity imparts a buoyant self-confidence which results in attractive games.

	White	*Black*
	LETELIER	FISCHER
1	P—Q4	N—KB3
2	P—QB4	P—KN3
3	N—QB3	B—N2
4	P—K4	....

And now, instead of playing the tried and true 4 . . . P—Q3, Black adopts a provocative novelty.

4	....	Castles!?

He dares White to advance his King Pawn.

5	P—K5	N—K1
6	P—B4	P—Q3
7	B—K3	....

DIAGRAM 83 Position after 7 B—K3

Black (FISCHER)

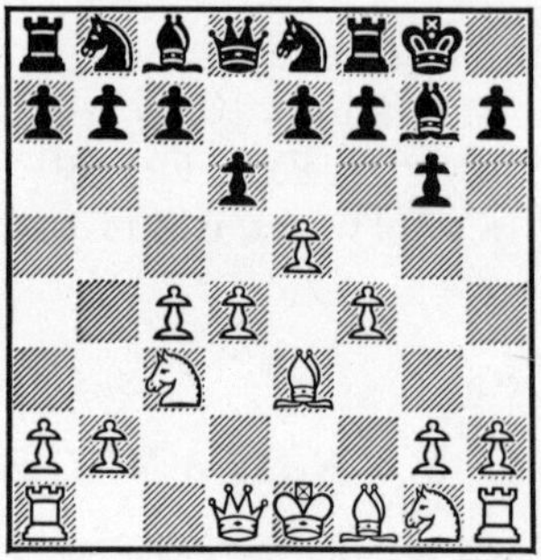

White (LETELIER)

About positions such as this one, there are two schools of thought. One holds that the advanced Pawn is weak and can be undermined by appropriate counterthrusts. The other maintains that Black has lost valuable time and that his pieces are constricted in their action.

The possibilities open to Black are a bit puzzling. He can try 7 . . . PxP in order to answer 8 BPxP with 8 . . . P—QB4! immediately smashing White's center. However, White can answer 7 . . . PxP with 8 QPxP! leaving Black with a clumsy position.

This explains why Black chooses a positional gambit instead.

7	. . . .	P—QB4!?
8	QPxP	N—QB3

A Pawn capture would of course cost Black his Queen.

9	BPxP	PxP

The position is becoming difficult for White, for example 10 PxP, NxP; 11 B—B5, R—K1 ch; 12 K—B2 (interposition at K2 allows . . . NxP), BxN!; 13 QxN (not 13 PxB?,

N—K5 ch winning a piece), QxQ; 14 BxQ, BxP and Black has regained his Pawn with a vastly superior game.

White's best course is to continue his development—say 10 N—B3, B—N5 (not 10 . . . PxP?; 11 B—B5 and White wins the exchange); 11 B—K2 and Black still has the problem of justifying his Pawn sacrifice; 11 . . . Q—R4 may be best.

10 N—K4? . . . .

Realizing that 10 . . . PxP? is ruled out by 11 B—B5 when White still wins the exchange, White pushes his luck too far.

10 . . . . B—B4!

This unexpected retort is based on the variation 11 NxP, NxN; 12 PxN, BxP and Black wins the exchange. Or 12 QxN, QxQ; 13 PxQ, BxP; 14 R—Q1, N—N5! and Black regains his Pawn favorably because of the double threat of . . . B—B7 or . . . NxP.

11 N—N3 B—K3!

Now White cannot very well play 12 PxP because of 12 . . . BxNP.

12 N—B3 Q—B2!

Tempting White to go in for 13 PxP, NxP; 14 B—B5, Q—R4 ch (of course, playing either Rook to Q1 is also good enough); 15 P—N4, NxNP; 16 BxN/Q6, N—Q6 dbl ch; 17 K—K2, BxP with a vicious attack.

DIAGRAM 84 Position after 12 . . . Q—B2!

Black (FISCHER)

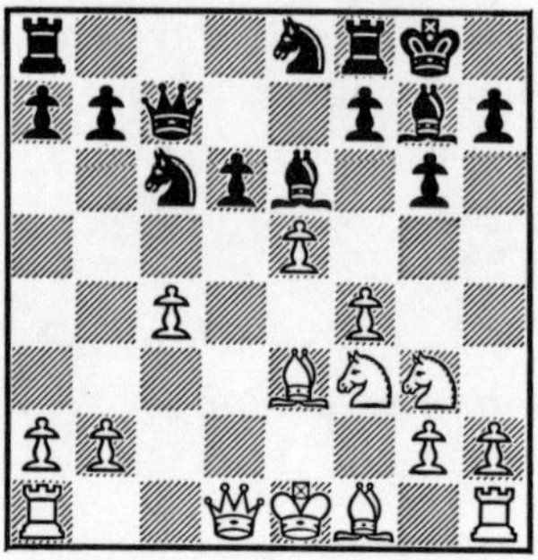

White (LETELIER)

13	Q—N1	. . . .

This queer-looking move is intended to defend White's Queen Knight Pawn after White's PxP. The Queen move also serves an aggressive purpose.

13	. . . .	PxP
14	P—KB5	. . . .

Realizing that after 14 PxP, NxP Black obtains a decisive initiative, White tries counterattack.

14	. . . .	P—K5!

Very fine. After 15 QxP, PxP!; 16 Q—R4 (not 16 NxP?, Q—R4 ch and Black wins a piece), Q—R4 ch; 17 B—Q2, Q—N3 the initiative is firmly in Black's hands.

15	PxB	PxN
16	NPxP	P—B4!

Threatens . . . P—B5.

17	P—B4	. . . .

Not 17 B—B5?, Q—K4 ch and Black wins a piece.

17	....	N—B3
18	B—K2	KR—K1
19	K—B2	....

Or 19 Castles, RxP and White is at a loss for a good move.

19	....	RxP
20	R—K1	QR—K1
21	B—B3	....

On the face of it, White has set up a sturdy defensive position. Actually Black has a brilliant winning line.

DIAGRAM 85 Position after 21 B—B3

Black (FISCHER)

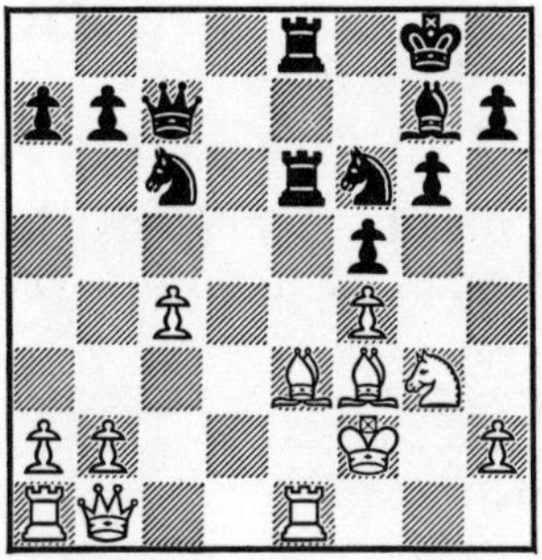

White (LETELIER)

21	....	RxB!
22	RxR	RxR
23	KxR	QxP ch!!
	Resigns	

For if 24 KxQ, B—R3 mate! Or 24 K—B2, N—K4; 25 Q—Q1, N/B3—N5 ch and Black either forces mate or wins the Queen.

47 *FRENCH DEFENSE*

INTERNATIONAL TEAM TOURNAMENT / LEIPZIG / 1960

To most of us a short, colorless draw is anathema, and rightly so. A game like the following one is something else again. Here we see two brilliant tacticians vie with each in a delightful display of pyrotechnics that winds up in a well-earned draw.

	White	*Black*
	FISCHER	TAL
1	P—K4	P—K3

An unusual defense for Tal.

2	P—Q4	P—Q4
3	N—QB3	B—N5
4	P—K5	. . . .

An exceedingly difficult variation which is rich in resources for both sides. Black naturally chooses the indicated counterthrust.

4	. . . .	P—QB4
5	P—QR3	B—R4!?

This leads to more tension than the old standard line 5 . . . BxN ch; 6 PxB which gives White a strong Pawn center and promising attacking chances.

6	P—QN4!?	. . . .

An ancient gambit line which goes back more than half a century.

In a Reshevsky-Botvinnik game, (Match U.S.A.-U.S.S.R. 1946) the continuation was 6 Q—N4, N—K2; 7 PxP, BxN ch; 8 PxB, N—Q2; 9 QxNP, KR—N1; 10 QxRP, Q—B2; 11 B—K2, NxKP; 12 B—Q2, QxP; 13 N—B3, NxN ch; 14 BxN, P—K4; 15 B—R5, B—B4! with a very complicated game and approximately equal chances.

6 .... PxQP!

Black is intent on breaking up White's Pawn center. White is therefore well advised to seek compensation in the form of a sharp attack.

DIAGRAM **86** Position after 6 . . . PxQP!

Black (TAL)

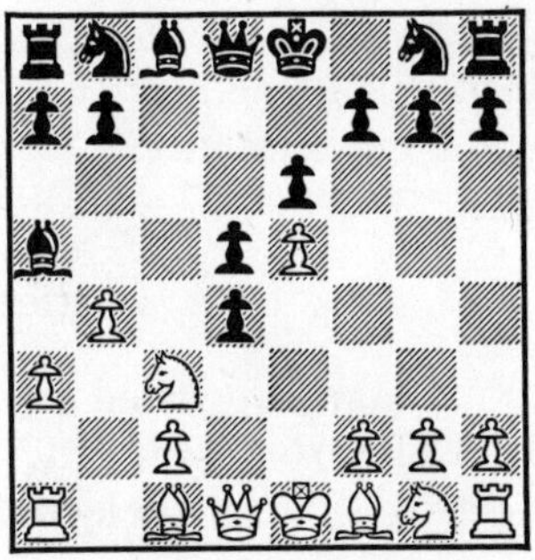

White (FISCHER)

7 Q—N4 ....

This is more promising than the older continuation 7 N—N5 etc.

7 .... N—K2!?

A two-Pawn sacrifice that has been favored by Soviet masters for many years.

8 PxB PxN
9 QxNP R—N1
10 QxRP QN—B3

Black is considerably ahead in development and, as he sees it, White's Queen is out of play. White, on the other hand, thinks of his Queen as aggressively posted; and his passed King Rook Pawn is a potential threat.

11 N—B3 ....

A hard choice. The alternative 11 P—B4 gives his King Pawn real security but at the cost of cutting down the mobility of his Queen Bishop—such moves as B—KN5 or B—KR6 are ruled out.

11	....	Q—B2
12	B—QN5!?	....

Offering a Pawn in order to pin White's Queen Knight. A plausible line now is 12 . . . RxP; 13 K—B1, KR—N1; 14 KR—N1!, RxR ch; 15 KxR. Now White threatens 16 N—N5 and Black must not play 15 . . . B—Q2?? for then 16 Q—R8 ch forces a quick mate!

12	....	B—Q2
13	Castles	Castles

After the game Petrosian suggested 13 . . . NxP; 14 NxN, QxN; 15 BxB ch, KxB; 16 Q—Q3, Q—K5. This seems preferable to the course actually selected by Black.

14	B—N5	....

White may have played this under the impression that he was thereby preventing 14 . . . NxP.

DIAGRAM 87 Position after 14 B—N5

Black (TAL)

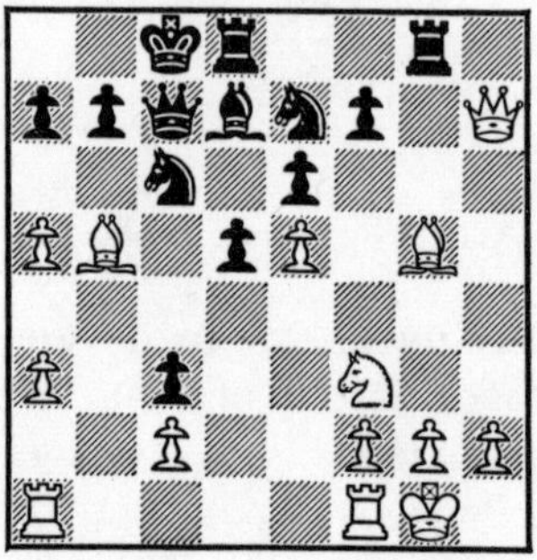

White (FISCHER)

14	....	NxP!

From here on it is fireworks all the way.

15	NxN!	....

Fischer took almost an hour on this move—a very unusual aspect of any of his games. Note that 15 BxN?, NxN ch; 16 K—R1, R—R1 would force White's resignation.

15	....	BxB

After 15 . . . QxN; 16 BxN, R—R1 White seems lost. But he creates a flight square for his King with 17 KR—K1! The sequel then might be 17 . . . QxR ch; 18 RxQ, RxQ; 19 BxR with a likely draw as the outcome.

16	NxP!	BxR!
17	NxR!	RxB!
18	NxP!	RxP ch!

Black has of course foreseen the consequences of this fine move. After 19 KxB he has the splendid resource 19 . . . RxRP!

19	K—R1!	....

White does not fear 19 . . . Q—QB5; 20 QxN, R—N1; 21 N—B4!

19	....	Q—K4!
20	RxB	....

Black can now try 20 . . . R—N3, but after 21 QxN, RxN; 22 Q—B5 ch a draw is in the cards anyway. So Black heads for an immediate perpetual check.

20	....	QxN
21	KxR	Q—N5 ch
	Drawn	

White cannot escape from the perpetual check. A delightful game.

48 *RUY LOPEZ*

ALEKHINE MEMORIAL TOURNAMENT / BLED / 1961

When players pride themselves on their originality, a very fine line will eventually be drawn between inspiration and eccentricity. In this game the player of the Black pieces palpably overreaches himself and in consequence receives a fearful drubbing from his alert but skeptical opponent.

	White	*Black*
	FISCHER	GELLER
1	P—K4	P—K4
2	N—KB3	N—QB3
3	B—N5	P—QR3
4	B—R4	P—Q3
5	Castles	B—N5

The first eccentricity. Instead, 5 . . . B—Q2 is normal, simple and satisfactory.

6	P—KR3	B—R4

Another step on the road to perdition. It was still possible for him to get on the right track with 6 . . . B—Q2.

7	P—B3	Q—B3?

A flagrant violation of basic opening principles. The premature development of Black's Queen immediately leads to trouble.

8	P—KN4!	. . . .

Though this looks risky, White has accurately weighed the resulting possibilities.

8	. . . .	B—N3

How should White protect his King Pawn?

DIAGRAM 88 Position after 8 . . . B—N3

Black (GELLER)

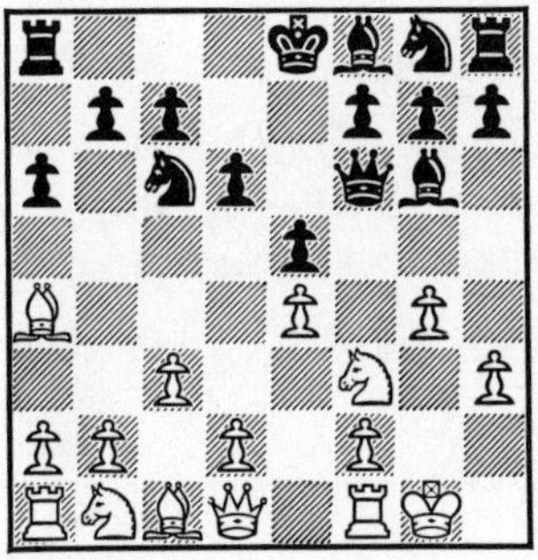

White (FISCHER)

9	P—Q4!	. . . .

White ignores the attack on his King Pawn—and with good reason.

He now has two threats: 10 P—Q5 attacking the Knight and also menacing 11 B—KN5 winning the Queen; the second threat is 10 B—KN5, Q—K3; 11 P—Q5 winning a piece.

9	. . . .	BxP

After 9 . . . P—N4; 10 B—B2, Q—Q1 (he has nothing better); 11 P—QR4 White has a clear initiative.

10	QN—Q2!	B—N3

The alternative 10 . . . BxN; 11 NxB, P—K5; 12 R—K1, P—Q4; 13 B—KN5! is anything but inviting.

11	BxN ch	PxB
12	PxP	PxP
13	NxP	. . . .

Since 13 . . . QxN? is ruled out by 14 R—K1, White has already regained his Pawn and still maintains the initiative.

13	....	B—Q3
14	NxB	QxN

Or 14 . . . RPxN; 15 N—K4!, Q—Q1; 16 R—K1 and White maintains lasting pressure.

15	R—K1 ch	K—B1

The alternative was 15 . . . N—K2; 16 N—B4, Castles/Q; 17 NxB ch, RxN; 18 Q—R4 and White wins a Pawn without allowing the Black King any real respite.

16	N—B4	P—KR4

A forlorn hope.

17	NxB	PxN

Or 17 . . . QxN; 18 QxQ ch, PxQ; 19 B—B4, R—Q1; 20 QR—Q1, P—Q4; 21 B—B7, R—Q2; 22 B—N6, N—R3; 23 P—B3 and White must win the ending.

18	B—B4	P—Q4

DIAGRAM 89 Position after 18 . . . P—Q4

Black (GELLER)

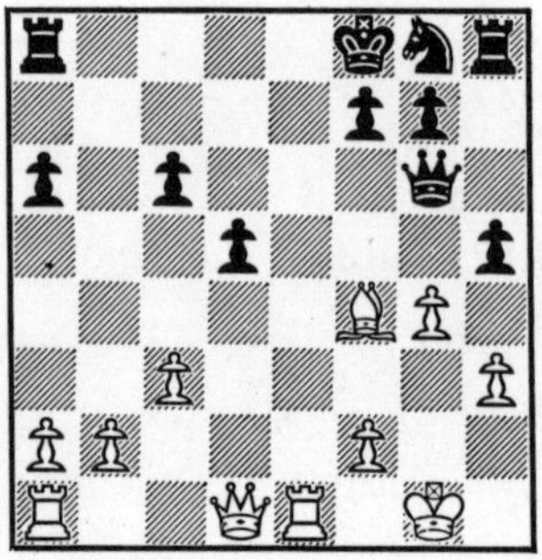

White (FISCHER)

19	Q—N3!	....

Now the win is clear. White threatens 20 Q—N4 ch (or 20 Q—R3 ch with the same effect) and also 20 Q—N7! The absence of Black's Queen proves disastrous to the end.

19	....	PxP

Surrender. However, if 19 . . . N—K2; 20 RxN!, KxR; 21 Q—N7 ch is deadly, while if 19 . . . N—B3; 20 Q—N7, R—K1; 21 RxR ch, NxR; 22 R—K1 and Black is lost.

20	Q—N7!	....

White is merciless, the move selected by him being even more powerful than an immediate Queen check.

20	....	PxP dis ch
21	B—N3	R—Q1

Or 21 . . . R—K1; 22 RxR ch, KxR; 23 R—K1 ch, finis.

22	Q—N4 ch!	Resigns

For now White picks up the Rook as well as the Knight. White's play has been artistic as well as logical.

49 *SICILIAN DEFENSE*

ALEKHINE MEMORIAL TOURNAMENT / BLED / 1961

The amusing feature of this game is that White plays it and wins it in the style of his redoubtable opponent. White's play throughout is most attractive, especially because of its deceptive air of effortlessness.

	White	*Black*
	FISCHER	TAL
1	P—K4	P—QB4
2	N—KB3	N—QB3

3	P—Q4	PxP
4	NxP	P—K3

By playing 4 . . . P—Q3 first, Black would have led into less dangerous lines. But Tal is not the man to avoid dangerous lines.

5	N—QB3	Q—B2

Black seems to be deliberately courting trouble. Here 5 . . . P—Q3 (or even 5 . . . P—QR3) would have been safer.

6	P—KN3	. . . .

This is played not merely to fianchetto his King Bishop—which, by the way, never happens—but also to play B—KB4 in some eventualities.

6	. . . .	N—B3?

Some critics have described this as the losing move, which is not too much of an exaggeration. It was essential to play 6 . . . P—QR3 here, to avoid the unpleasant line which is now unfolded.

DIAGRAM 90 Position after 6 . . . N—B3?

Black (TAL)

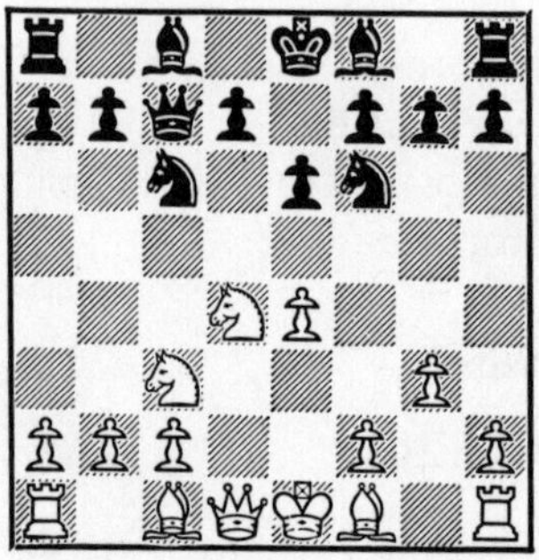

White (FISCHER)

7	N/Q4—N5	Q—N1

This clumsy retreat is virtually forced, as the more prosaic 7 . . . Q—Q1 would be answered by 8 N—Q6 ch, leaving Black with a strategically lost game.

8	B—KB4!	. . . .

Retribution for Black's sins. His "best" reply is 8 . . . P—K4; 9 B—N5! (in order to remove Black's protective Knight so that White can occupy the Q5 square with powerful effect), P—QR3; 10 BxN, PxB; 11 N—R3, BxN; 12 PxB with a wild position that distinctly favors White.

8	. . . .	N—K4

Tricky. Maybe White will play 9 Q—Q4??, N—B6 ch; 10 K—Q1, NxQ; 11 BxQ, NxN and Black wins a piece.

9	B—K2!	. . . .

This rules out . . . N—B6 ch in reply to Q—Q4, so that move is now a serious threat. White correctly decides that B—K2 is stronger than the more plausible 9 B—N2. This Bishop is more useful in the center.

9	. . . .	B—B4

A move that has been criticized, but the alternative 9 . . . P—QR3; 10 Q—Q4!, P—Q3; 11 Castles/Q! is at least as grim for Black.

10	BxN!	. . . .

An amazing move, and an amazingly simple move. What makes the move difficult to foresee is that it seems to ease Black's problems. Actually, as we shall see, they now become more acute.

10	. . . .	QxB
11	P—B4	Q—N1
12	P—K5	. . . .

DIAGRAM 91 Position after 12 P—K5

Black (TAL)

White (FISCHER)

Now the full strength of White's surprising tenth move is revealed. After 12 . . . N—N1; 13 N—K4 White is bound to sink one of his Knights on the Q6 square, leaving Black with a hopeless game.

12	....	P—QR3

This leads to complications that are decidedly in White's favor.

13	PxN	PxN
14	PxP	R—N1
15	N—K4	B—K2
16	Q—Q4	R—R5
17	N—B6 ch	BxN

And not 17 . . . K—Q1?; 18 NxR, RxQ; 19 N—R6 followed by 20 P—N8/Q ch and White is a Rook ahead.

18	QxB	....

With at least three brutal threats: 19 B—R5, or 19 Q—R6, or 19 B—Q3.

18	....	Q—B2

This holds the position together, though only momentarily.

If White plays 19 B—R5 Black has a defense in 19 . . . P—Q4. And on 19 Q—R6 Black has 19 . . . QxQBP.

The most complicated possibility is 19 B—Q3, analyzed in this fashion by Kmoch: 19 . . . Q—B4; 20 BxRP?, Q—K6 ch; 21 K—B1 forced, Q—KB6 ch; 22 K—N1, Q—K6 ch; 23 K—N2, Q—K7 ch; 24 K—R3, RxNP!; 25 QxR, Q—R4 ch and Black draws by perpetual check.

19	Castles/Q!	RxP
20	K—N1	. . . .

The simplest. If Black replies 20 . . . Q—R4 White parries the threat of 21 . . . R—R8 mate by simply playing 22 P—N3! In that event the threat of 22 B—Q3 or 22 B—R5 is ruinous for Black.

20	. . . .	R—R3
21	BxP	R—N3
22	B—Q3	. . . .

Black must find something against the threat of 23 BxP.

22	. . . .	P—K4

He is content with the lost but probably long-drawn-out ending that will result from 23 QxKP ch, QxQ; 24 PxQ, RxKNP. But Fischer has an admirable surprise in store for him.

DIAGRAM 92 Position after 22 . . . P—K4

Black (TAL)

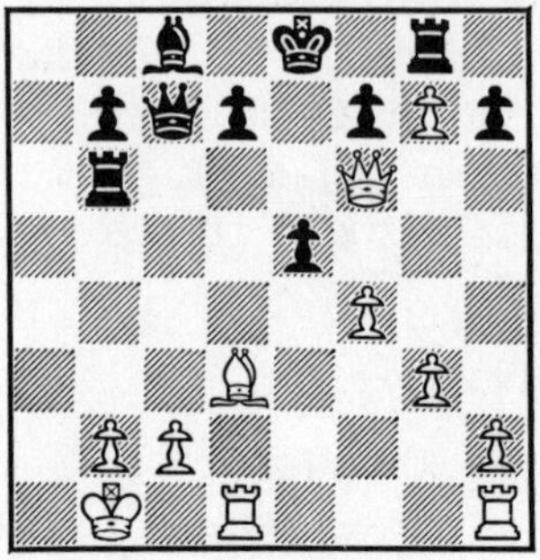

White (FISCHER)

23	PxP!!	. . . .

Very pretty—not that White is really "sacrificing," as he gets more than enough for the Queen.

23	. . . .	RxQ
24	PxR	Q—B4

Forced, for on such moves as 24 . . . Q—B3 or 24 . . . Q—N3 White plays 25 KR—B1! and Black has no defense to the coming 26 BxP.

25	BxP	. . . .

In the event of 25 KR—B1 Black has 25 . . . RxP; 26 PxR, Q—KN4 disposing of the remaining formidable Pawn.

25	. . . .	Q—KN4

Now, too, 26 KR—B1 would be no improvement on White's play because of 26 . . . RxP etc.

26	BxR	QxBP
27	KR—B1!	. . . .

Much stronger than 27 B—R7, QxKNP etc.

27	....	QxKNP
28	BxP ch	K—Q1

Naturally 28 . . . QxB; 29 RxQ, KxR leaves Black with a hopeless inferiority in material. The ensuing ending is conducted very ably by White.

29	B—K6	....

White threatens 30 R—B7, Q—N3; 31 BxP! while 31 . . . QxR is refuted by 32 B—K6 dis ch. Even simpler, however, was 29 R—Q3 followed by the steady advance of his Rook Pawn.

29	....	Q—R3

This enables Black to pick up one of the passed Pawns, whereas after 29 . . . K—B2; 30 B—B5 White would have time to guard his King-side Pawns and win easily by advancing them.

30	BxP	BxB
31	R—B7	QxP
32	R/Q1xB ch	K—K1
33	R/Q7—K7 ch	K—Q1
34	R—Q7 ch	K—B1
35	R—B7 ch	K—Q1
36	R/KB7—Q7 ch	K—K1
37	R—Q1	....

The more obvious 37 RxP is also good enough. White has various ways to win.

37	....	P—N4

After 37 . . . QxNP; 38 R—R1 mate threats begin to appear.

38	R—QN7	Q—R4

Or 38 . . . QxP; 39 R—R1, Q—K4; 40 R—R8 ch!, QxR; 41 R—N8 ch winning the Queen.

DIAGRAM 93 Position after 38 . . . Q—R4

Black (TAL)

White (FISCHER)

39	P—KN4!	Q—R6

The alternative 39 . . . QxP allows 40 R—R1, Q—Q5; 41 R—R8 ch!

40	P—N5	Q—KB6
41	R—K1 ch	K—B1
42	RxP	K—N2

All is lost save honor.

43	R—N6	Q—KN6
44	R—Q1	Q—B2

Or 44 . . . QxP; 45 R—Q7 ch and White forces mate.

45	R/Q1—Q6	Q—B1
46	P—N3	K—R2
47	R—QR6!	Resigns

White threatens to take the seventh rank again. If Black prevents this by 47 . . . Q—B2 or 47 . . . Q—N2 White wins the Queen with 48 R—R6 ch, K—N2; 49 R/QR6—N6 ch, K—B1; 50 R—R8 ch etc. This game was played in superior style by Fischer throughout.

50 *SICILIAN DEFENSE*

ALEKHINE MEMORIAL TOURNAMENT / BLED / 1961

In positions where a player exerts strong pressure on his opponent's game, there comes a moment when bold action will carry off the victory while hesitation will forfeit all or most of the advantage. This time we have a prime example of precise evaluation, a bold conclusion, and relentless exploitation of the advantage.

	White	*Black*
	FISCHER	OLAFSSON
1	P—K4	P—QB4
2	N—KB3	P—KN3
3	P—Q4	PxP
4	NxP	B—N2
5	N—QB3	N—QB3
6	B—K3	N—B3
7	B—QB4	....

Fischer's favorite move in the Sicilian, as we know from earlier games. He soon decides, however, that the Bishop is better off at K2.

7	....	Q—R4

Nor is this a happy spot for the Black Queen; but the threat of 8 . . . NxP gives the move a temporary validity.

8	Castles	P—Q3
9	N—N3	Q—B2
10	B—K2	....

Black was about to play 10 . . . N—K4. If White prevented this with 11 P—B4, the reply 11 . . . N—KN5 would have been annoying. So White decides that K2 is the better square for the Bishop after all.

10	....	Castles
11	P—B4	P—QR4

A doubtful move, as it weakens the squares QN3 and QN4 in Black's camp.

12	P—QR4	N—QN5
13	R—B2!	P—K4?!

A daring conception. White's Knights are to be deprived of access to his Q4 square, but the weakness of Black's Queen Pawn is an expensive price to pay for this. The familiar maneuver . . . B—K3—B5 is indicated.

14	B—B3	B—Q2
15	R—Q2!	....

White loses no time in fastening his attention on the weak Pawn.

15	....	KR—Q1

For Black can answer 16 RxP with 16 . . . BxP!

16	K—R1!	....

A subtle and powerful move which at this moment looks meaningless.

16	....	B—B3

DIAGRAM 94 Position after 16 . . . B—B3

Black (OLAFSSON)

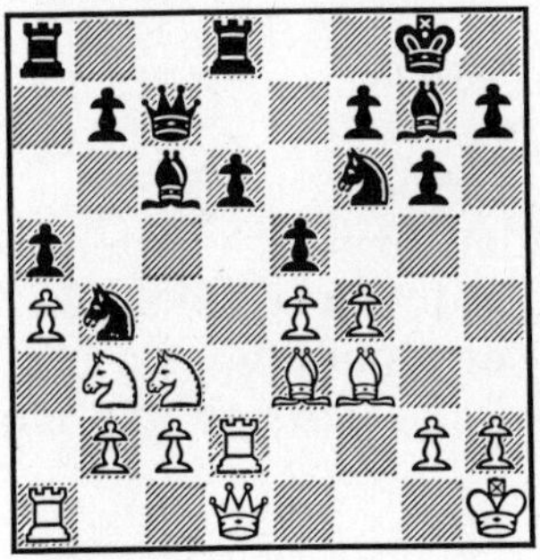

White (FISCHER)

17	Q—KN1!	. . . .

By "castling with his Queen" White threatens B—N6 and makes room for the doubling of his Rooks on the Queen file.

17	. . . .	N—Q2

Black is now on the point of getting a game of sorts with . . . PxP followed by . . . N—K4. White spikes this idea at once.

18	P—B5!	P—N3

In order to establish a Knight at his QB4 square.

19	QR—Q1	N—B4
20	N—N5	Q—K2

This leads to complications which ultimately turn out to White's advantage; 20 . . . BxN may have been the lesser evil.

21	NxQP	NxBP
22	NxN	NxB
23	QxN	PxN
24	B—K2	. . . .

Though this move turns out well, the more conservative 24 P—QN3 seems more logical as a preliminary to the maneuver B—K2—B4.

24	....	BxRP
25	P—QN3	B—K1
26	B—B4	P—R5

A difficult situation for Black. After 26 . . . Q—R2, for example, there might follow 27 BPxP, KRPxP; 28 R—KB1, R—Q2; 29 NxB (or simply 29 B—N5! winning the exchange), RxN; 30 RxR, QxR; 31 RxP and wins.

DIAGRAM 95 Position after 26 . . . P—R5

Black (OLAFSSON)

White (FISCHER)

27	B—Q5!	....

Creating further difficulties for Black. After the plausible reply 27 . . . R—R2 the continuation might be 28 NxB, RxN (if 28 . . . QxN; 29 BxP ch etc.); 29 BPxP, KRPxP; 30 R—KB2, Q—B1; 31 PxP and White has all the play.

27	....	RxN!?

This sacrifice of the exchange is almost good enough to extricate Black from his troubles.

28	BxR	R—Q5

The occupation of this strong point is a big asset for Black, but Fischer finds an extraordinary way to nullify it.

29	BPxP!	....

Pressure along the King Bishop file is the key to White's plan.

29	....	KRPxP
30	PxP	BxP
31	R—R1	Q—B1

Black threatens . . . B—R3 as well as . . . QxB. But White has seen further ahead; above all he avoids 32 RxR, KPxR; 33 Q—QR3, QxB; 34 QxB, QxQ; 35 RxQ, P—Q6 and Black wins.

DIAGRAM 96 Position after 31 . . . Q—B1

Black (OLAFSSON)

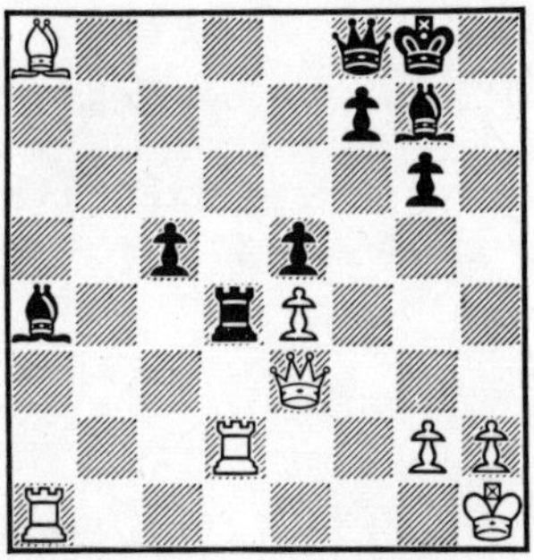

White (FISCHER)

32	B—Q5!	B—R3
33	RxR	....

The indicated sequel.

33	....	BxQ
34	R/Q4xB	....

Threatens to win Black's Queen with R—R8.

34	....	Q—R3
35	R—KB1!	....

Now White threatens to win with 36 R—R8 ch, K—R2; 37 RxP ch etc.

35	....	B—B5

Black wards off the threat and in turn threatens mate. But White has a splendid resource.

36	P—N3!	....

For if 36 . . . BxP (still threatening mate), White wins with 37 R—R8 ch etc.

36	....	Q—R6
37	R/R4—R1!	....

This retreat lends a charming artistic touch to the attack.

37	....	BxP
38	R—R8 ch!	Resigns

For after 38 . . . K—N2; 39 RxP ch, K—R3; 40 R—R8 ch White wins the Queen. A fitting conclusion to an embittered struggle.

51 *KING'S INDIAN DEFENSE*

ALEKHINE MEMORIAL TOURNAMENT / BLED / 1961

Another drawn game in which both masters give of their best. The delightful middle game play, in which the players vie with each other in sharp thrust and parry, is especially rewarding.

	White	*Black*
	GLIGORIC	FISCHER
1	P—Q4	N—KB3
2	P—QB4	P—KN3
3	N—QB3	B—N2
4	P—K4	P—Q3
5	N—B3	Castles
6	B—K2	P—K4
7	Castles	....

Regarding an attempt to win a Pawn with 7 PxP, see Game 38.

7	....	N—B3
8	P—Q5	N—K2

Black takes the view that it is well worth losing time with his Knight moves in order to get in the counterthrust with . . . P—KB4.

9	N—K1	....

White too has his special reasons for wanting to advance his King Bishop Pawn.

9	....	N—Q2
10	N—Q3	P—KB4
11	PxP	NxBP

This Knight will occupy his Q5 square, from which it can never be driven away by a White Pawn.

DIAGRAM 97 Position after 11 . . . NxBP

Black (FISCHER)

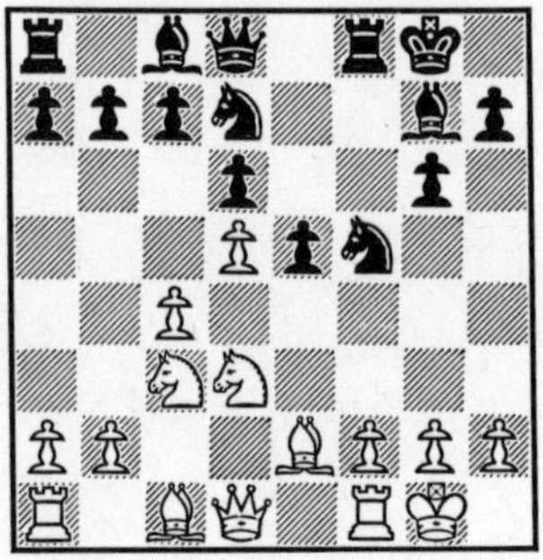

White (GLIGORIC)

White wants to occupy his K4 square, but since his Queen Knight is already well placed, he prefers to use his other Knight for this purpose. This calls for P—B3 followed by N—B2—K4.

12	P—B3	N—B3
13	N—B2	N—Q5
14	N/B2—K4	N—R4
15	B—N5	Q—Q2!

This surprising move (blocking the development of his Queen Bishop) turns out to have some subtle points.

16	P—KN3	. . . .

White is determined to prevent . . . N—B5; but Black is not without clever counterattacking resources.

16	. . . .	P—KR3
17	B—K3	P—B4!

There is more to this move than meets the eye, as it involves the sacrifice of two Pawns.

18	BxN	KPxB
19	N—QN5	. . . .

This settles the fate of Black's Pawn at Queen 3: 19 . . . B—K4 is useless because of 20 P—B4.

19 . . . . P—R3!

Black initiates a deep combination.

20 N/N5xP P—Q6!

The necessary sequel. If now 21 NxB?, PxB! wins.

21 QxP B—Q5 ch

DIAGRAM 98 Position after 21 .. . B—Q5 ch

Black (FISCHER)

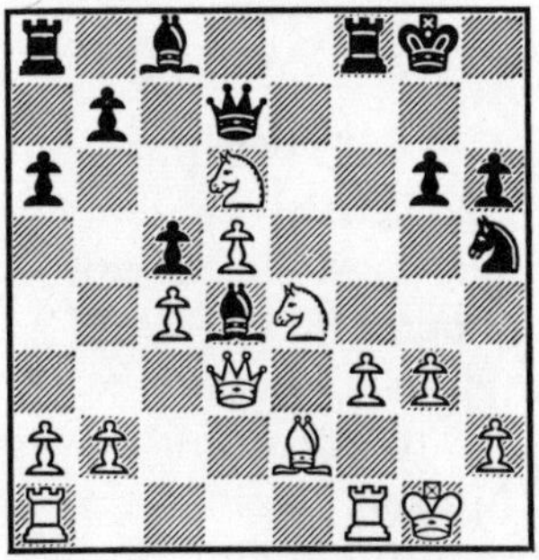

White (GLIGORIC)

Now Black's idea becomes clear. On 22 K—R1 there follows 22 . . . NxP ch!; 23 NxN (not 23 PxN??, Q—R6 mate), QxN and Black's aggressive position, backed by the two Bishops, is well worth a Pawn.

22 K—N2! NxP!

For 23 KxN?? or 23 PxN?? allows 23 . . . Q—R6 mate.

23 NxB! . . . .

Much more promising than 23 NxN, QxN etc.

23	....	NxR!
24	N—N6	Q—QB2!

Leaving White no time for 25 NxR?? because of the reply 25 . . . QxP ch and mate next move.

25	RxN!	....

Stronger than 25 BxN, as he is preparing the advance of his Queen Knight Pawn.

25	....	QxN
26	P—N4!	....

Despite his loss of the exchange White has a powerful position after this thrust. The immediate threat is 27 PxP, BxP; 28 NxB, QxN; 29 QxP ch with a draw by perpetual check.

26	....	QxP

In the event of 26 . . . PxP White continues 27 P—B5!, BxP; 28 NxB, QxN; 29 QxP ch etc.

A more complicated possibility is 26 . . . K—R1; 27 PxP, BxP; 28 R—QN1! (not 28 NxB?, QxN; 29 QxP??, R—KN1 and White's Queen is lost), Q—R2; 29 NxB, QxN; 30 RxP and White threatens to force mate with 31 Q—B3 ch. Black can defend himself against this threat but only at the cost of allowing White's Pawns to advance (31 . . . Q—Q3; 32 P—B5!, QxBP?; 33 QxNP, R—KN1; 34 R—R7 mate. Or 31 . . . R—B3; 32 Q—B3, Q—KB1; 33 P—B5 or 33 R—N6 etc.).

DIAGRAM 99 Position after 26 . . . QxP

Black (FISCHER)

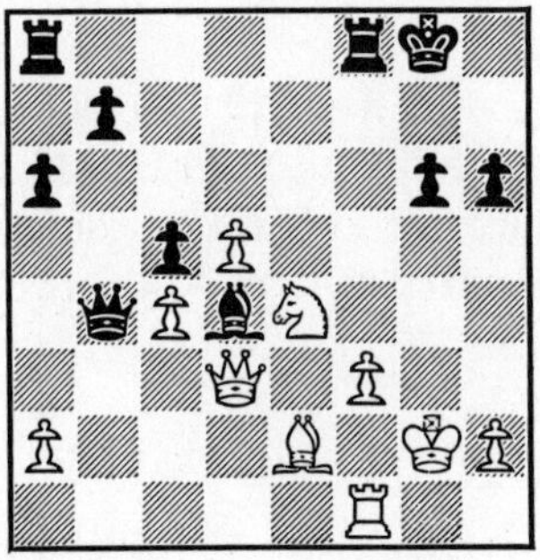

White (GLIGORIC)

27	R—QN1	Q—R4
28	NxP!	QxN

Not 28 . . . BxN?; 29 QxP ch, K—R1; 30 RxP and Black is lost (30 . . . R—KN1; 31 R—R7 mate).

29	QxP ch	B—N2
30	RxP	Q—Q5
31	B—Q3!	R—B5

Here 31 . . . KR—K1 allows the draw by 32 Q—B7 ch, K—R1; 33 Q—N6 etc. while 31 . . . R—B3?? allows 32 QxB mate.

32	Q—K6 ch	K—R1

Not 32 . . . K—B1?; 33 B—R7! and White wins.

33	Q—KN6	Drawn

Both sides must be content with the draw (33 . . . K—N1; 34 Q—K6 ch etc.). A fascinating battle.

52 CARO-KANN DEFENSE

INTERZONAL TOURNAMENT / STOCKHOLM / 1962

White starts out with a slight but perceptible theoretical advantage which he exploits relentlessly to achieve an impressive victory. Barcza relies on his dour, dry style only to find that he is no match for his youthful, less experienced opponent.

	White	*Black*
	FISCHER	BARCZA
1	P—K4	P—QB3
2	N—QB3	P—Q4
3	N—B3	PxP
4	NxP	N—B3
5	NxN ch	KPxN

Here is White's theoretical advantage. Black is left with four Pawns to three on the King-side, but his extra Pawn there can never be converted into a passed Pawn because his King-side Pawns are doubled. In addition, these Pawns may become weak in the endgame.

On the other hand, White's four Pawns to three constitute a real majority from which a passed Pawn can be fashioned.

One more important point: simplification favors White. The more pieces that are exchanged, the easier it will be for him to utilize his Pawn majority.

DIAGRAM 100 Position after 5 . . . KPxN

Black (BARCZA)

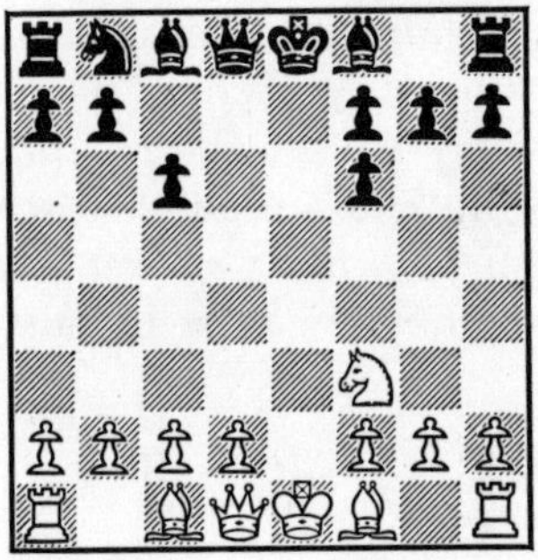

White (FISCHER)

6	P—Q4	B—Q3
7	B—QB4	Castles
8	Castles	R—K1
9	B—N3	. . . .

Apparently with the idea of advancing his Queen Bishop Pawn to mobilize the Pawn majority. If this is his intention, he soon changes his mind.

9	. . . .	N—Q2
10	N—R4	N—B1
11	Q—Q3	. . . .

White wants to provoke . . . P—KN3 (to keep the White Knight out), for he realizes that any move of the Pawns will create a weakness that can be exploited later on in the endgame stage.

11	. . . .	B—B2

Following the same reasoning, Black tries to avoid moving one of the Pawns.

12	B—K3	Q—K2

Black realizes that the mating threat 12 . . . Q—Q3 can be parried easily enough with 13 P—KN3.

13	N—B5	....

Confronting Black with a number of disagreeable alternatives: he can leave this Knight at its powerful post by retreating his Queen and remaining in an uncomfortably cramped position in which White has all the positional trumps; or he can play 13 . . . Q—K5, playing into White's hands by engineering the simplification that White aims for, or he can play 13 . . . BxN giving White the positional advantage of two Bishops against Bishop and Knight.

13	....	Q—K5
14	QxQ	RxQ
15	N—N3	R—K1

The alternative 15 . . . BxN; 16 RPxB would leave White with two Bishops against Bishop and Knight, always a considerable positional advantage in such situations.

DIAGRAM 101 Position after 15 . . . R—K1

Black (BARCZA)

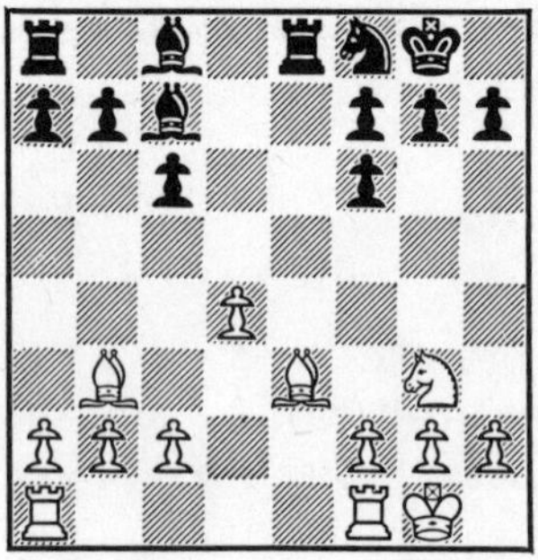

White (FISCHER)

16	P—Q5!	....

The positional turning point. If Black exchanges Pawns, White's King Bishop becomes very powerful. If Black tries to hedge with 16 . . . B—Q2 then 17 QR—Q1 (possibly with a view to P—Q6, creating a formidable passed Pawn) maintains the pressure.

16	....	PxP
17	BxQP	....

Black's difficulties have intensified. If he tries 17 . . . B—Q2; 18 BxNP, QR—N1; 19 B—Q5, RxP his Rook is boxed in by 20 B—N3! with considerable advantage to White.

17	....	B—N3

Black tries another way, but he now acquires a new set of doubled Pawns—and isolated at that. An ominous development.

18	BxB	PxB

As a consolation prize Black has obtained an open file for his Queen Rook.

19	P—QR3	....

Note hereabouts that White is in no hurry to mobilize his Queen-side Pawn majority. He is content to preserve this valuable asset for the later endgame stage.

19	....	R—R4
20	QR—Q1	R—B4

But not 20 . . . R—Q1?; 21 BxBP ch and White wins. Meanwhile Black's remaining Bishop is paralyzed.

21	P—QB3	R—B2
22	B—B3!	R—Q2

Or 22 . . . B—Q2; 23 R—Q6 and White's pressure is unabated.

23	RxR	NxR

Forced. But now White's Knight makes a powerful entry.

24	N—B5!	N—B4

No better was 24 . . . N—K4; 25 N—Q6!, NxB ch; 26 PxN, R—Q1; 27 NxB, RxN; 28 R—Q1!, K—B1; 29 R—Q6, R—B3; 30 R—Q7 and White wins a Pawn.

25	N—Q6!	R—Q1
26	NxB	RxN
27	R—Q1!	. . . .

Much stronger than 27 P—QN4, N—R5 and Black has counterplay. If now 27 . . . N—R5; 28 R—Q2 and White's winning of a Pawn is only a question of time.

27	. . . .	K—B1
28	R—Q4	. . . .

Threatening to win a Pawn with 29 R—QN4.

28	. . . .	R—B2

Black protects the Pawn at QN2 so that he can be ready to answer 29 R—QN4 with 29 . . . N—Q2.

DIAGRAM 102 Position after 28 . . . R—B2

Black (BARCZA)

White (FISCHER)

29	P—R3!	. . . .

Here 29 K—B1 would have been equally good. The point of these moves is that after 29 R—QN4, N—Q2; 30 B—N4

(apparently winning a Pawn) Black can defend for the time being with 30 . . . P—N3; 31 K—B1 (not 30 BxN, RxB; 31 RxP??, R—Q8 mate), P—B4 etc.

29	....	P—B4

Now that the potential mating threat has been lifted, Black must prevent 31 B—N4 after 30 R—QN4, N—Q2.

30	R—QN4	N—Q2
31	K—B1	....

White's King heads for a notable role in the center.

31	....	K—K2

While Black's King rushes to defend his weak Pawn at QN2.

32	K—K2	K—Q1
33	R—N5!	....

Forces another weakness in Black's Pawn position and also prepares for moves 38–39.

33	....	P—N3
34	K—K3	K—B1
35	K—Q4	K—N1
36	K—Q5	....

White threatens to reduce his opponent to helplessness: for example, 36 . . . K—B1; 37 K—Q6, K—Q1; 38 B—Q5, N—B3; 39 P—QB4 etc. Black therefore decides to make a stand on the third rank.

36	....	R—B3
37	K—Q4	R—K3

On 37 . . . R—B2; 38 B—Q5 is very strong.

38	P—QR4!	....

In order to push this Pawn on, since . . . PxP will be out of the question.

38	....	K—B2
39	P—R5!	R—Q3 ch

Obviously not 39 . . . PxP; 40 RxNP ch followed by R—R7 winning the Queen Rook Pawn easily.

40	B—Q5	....

DIAGRAM 103 Position after 40 B—Q5

Black (BARCZA)

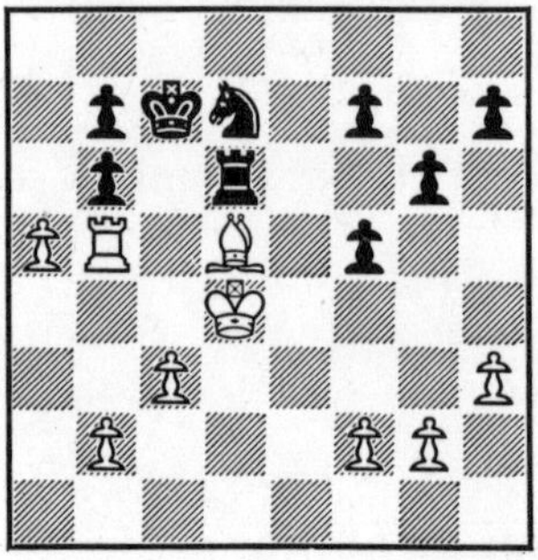

White (FISCHER)

As Kmoch demonstrates, Black can no longer rely on passive defense: 40 . . . R—KB3; 41 P—KB4, R—Q3; 42 P—B4, R—KB3; 43 PxP ch, NxP; 44 B—B3, R—Q3 ch; 45 K—B3 and White must win.

Here are some of the likely possibilities: 45 . . . R—KB3; 46 P—B5! followed by 47 RxP ch etc. Or 45 . . . P—B3; 46 P—B5, N—Q4 ch; 47 K—Q4! and White wins a piece. Or 45 . . . K—B1; 46 BxP ch!, KxB; 47 P—B5 forcing a won King and Pawn ending: 47 . . . R—QB3; 48 RxN ch, RxR; 49 PxR, KxP; 50 K—Q4, K—B3; 51 K—K5 etc. or 50 . . . P—B3; 52 K—Q5 etc. This last line is a perfect example of the Pawn-majority theory expounded in the opening note: White massacres Black's King-side Pawns while the Black King is held back by White's passed Queen Knight Pawn.

40	....	K—B1
41	PxP	P—B3

Or 41 . . . NxP; 42 K—K5, K—B2; 43 R—B5 ch!, K—Q2; 44 BxNP!, R—Q7; 45 P—QN4 and White's passed Pawns are irresistible. Again the Pawn majority proves its value.

42	K—K3!	....

White unpins his Bishop to head for a new target: Black's vulnerable King-side Pawns.

42	....	NxP

Equally distasteful is 42 . . . RxP; 43 RxR, NxR; 44 B—N8, P—N4 (if 44 . . . N—R5; 45 BxP, NxNP; 46 BxP with an easy win); 45 BxP, P—B5 ch; 46 K—K4, K—Q2 (if 46 . . . N—R5; 47 K—B5 etc.); 47 P—QN3 and White wins as he pleases.

43	B—N8	K—B2

He sees that 43 . . . P—R3 is futile because of 44 B—R7 etc.

44	R—B5 ch	K—N1
45	BxP	N—Q4 ch
46	K—B3	N—K2
47	P—R4!	....

An echo of the maneuver with the other Rook Pawn. P—R5 will win another Pawn—at least.

47	....	P—N3
48	R—N5	K—N2
49	P—R5!	K—R3
50	P—B4	PxP
51	BxP	R—Q5

Or 51 . . . NxB; 52 RxN and White picks up a second Pawn.

52	P—QN3	N—B3
53	K—K3	R—Q1
54	B—K4	N—R4

If 54 . . . N—K4; 55 R—N4 (threatening mate) wins more material.

55	B—B2	P—R5

On 55 . . . R—KR1; 56 R—KB5, R—R3 White can win in various ways—for example, by bringing his King to KR4.

56	R—R5	R—K1 ch
57	K—Q2	R—KN1
58	RxP	P—N4

Equally hopeless is 58 . . . RxP; 59 R—B4 because Black cannot play 59 . . . R—N3.

59	R—B4	. . . .

Another way is 59 PxP ch, KxP; 60 P—N3.

59	. . . .	PxP
60	PxP	RxP

If 60 . . . R—KB1 White continues P—N4-5 after shielding his King from check.

61	RxP ch	K—R2
62	K—B3	R—N5
63	P—B4	N—N2
64	K—N4	Resigns

The advance of the Queen Bishop Pawn will be deadly (the final utilization of the Queen-side majority). A masterly ending by White.

53 *SICILIAN DEFENSE*

INTERZONAL TOURNAMENT / STOCKHOLM / 1962

The great American masters of the past, by and large, had little use for the fine points of opening play. They paid comparatively slight attention to formal variations and were content to improvise their analysis over the board.

Fischer is of a different breed. He spends many hours on his "homework," painstakingly reviewing the findings of other analysts and drawing his own conclusions. This is quite obvious in the following game, in which he confidently selects an inordinately difficult variation and requires only seven minutes for twenty-three of the most trying moves ever made in a game of chess.

	White	*Black*
	BILEK	FISCHER
1	P—K4	P—QB4
2	N—KB3	P—Q3
3	P—Q4	PxP
4	NxP	N—KB3
5	N—QB3	P—QR3
6	B—KN5	....

After 6 B—K2 the reply would doubtless have been 6 . . . P—K4, as in Game 37.

6	....	P—K3
7	P—B4	Q—N3

Black varies from 7 . . . B—K2; 8 Q—B3, Q—B2 (played in Games 40 and 43).

DIAGRAM 104 Position after 7 . . . Q—N3

Black (FISCHER)

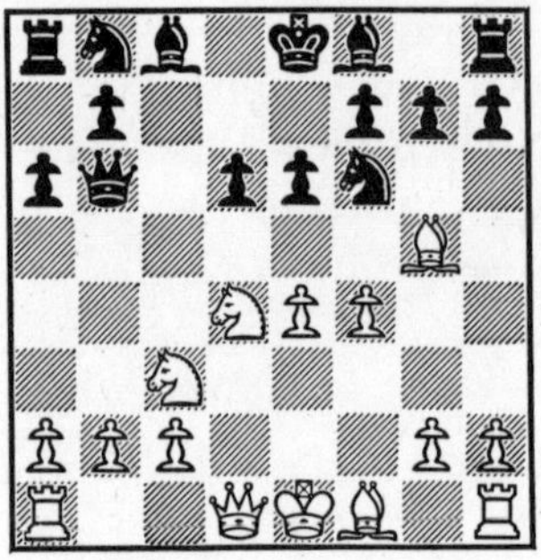

White (BILEK)

White must now decide whether he wishes to protect his Queen Knight Pawn with 8 N—N3 with the likely sequel 8 . . . Q—K6 ch; 9 Q—K2, QxQ ch; 10 BxQ etc. or whether he should sacrifice the Pawn with 8 Q—Q2!?

In the first case White obtains a greater command of the board and a lead in development, though Black's game is quite solid. In the second case we get a wild attack in which pieces are sacrificed in the most nonchalant manner.

8	Q—Q2!?	QxP!?

Consistent but very dangerous.

9	QR—N1	Q—R6

In a Parma-Fischer game (Bled, 1961) the continuation was 10 BxN, PxB; 11 B—K2, N—B3; 12 N—N3, B—N2; 13 P—B5, Castles; 14 Castles, N—K4; 15 N—Q4, P—N4; 16 K—R1, B—Q2; 17 B—R5! and Black's position became progressively more difficult.

10	P—K5	. . . .

The main line, and a very dangerous one for Black, as transpired in the earliest game with this variation: 10 . . .

KN—Q2?; 11 P—B5!, NxP; 12 PxP, PxP; 13 B—K2!, QN—B3; 14 NxN, PxN; 15 N—K4!, P—Q4; 16 Castles, Q—R5; 17 B—R5 ch, K—Q2; 18 RxB!, resigns (Keres-Fuderer, Gothenburg, 1955).

10	....	PxP
11	PxP	KN—Q2

If White tries to strengthen the attack with 12 N—K4 the sequel might be 12 . . . P--R3; 13 B—R4, QxP; 14 R—N3, QN—B3; 15 NxN, PxN; 16 N—Q6 ch, BxN; 17 QxB, Q—R4 ch! and Black forces the exchange of Queens.

12	B—QB4	....

The story goes that during postmortem analysis of his Bled game with Parma, Fischer was asked by Naidorf what he would have played in this position. Fischer is supposed to have replied: "That's a secret." In this game the secret is revealed.

12	....	B—K2
13	BxKP!?	....

Now the game gets very wild. Black's acceptance of the sacrifice might lead to the following: 13 . . . PxB; 14 NxP, BxB; 15 N—B7 ch, K—Q1; 16 QxB ch, KxN; 17 N—Q5 ch, K—B3 and now White can draw with 18 N—K7 ch etc. or try for a win with 18 P—K6 etc.

If, instead, 13 . . . BxB; 14 BxP ch!, KxB; 15 Castles ch or 14 . . . K—B1; 15 N—K6 ch, KxB; 16 NxB ch, White has a winning attack.

DIAGRAM 105 Position after 13 BxKP!?

Black (FISCHER)

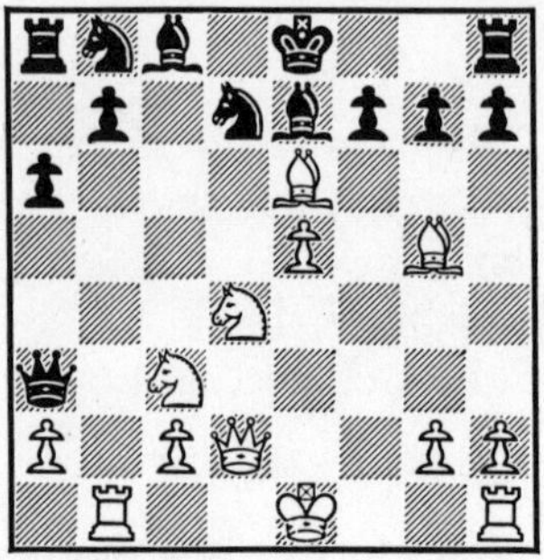

White (BILEK)

13	....	Castles
14	Castles!?	BxB!

An improvement on Dueckstein-Euwe (Chaumont, 1958) which continued 14 . . . PxB?; 15 NxP, N—QB3; 16 N—Q5!, B—B4 ch; 17 K—R1, N/B3xP; 18 NxR, BxN; 19 N—B7 and White had a winning attack.

15	QxB	....

If now 15 . . . QxN?; 16 N—B5, P—KN3; 17 Q—R6, QxKP (if 17 . . . PxN; 18 BxP/B5 and Black is lost); 18 N—K7 ch, K—R1; 19 NxP ch, PxN; 20 RxR ch, NxR; 21 QxN mate.

Or 15 . . . QxN?; 16 N—B5, QxKP; 17 N—R6 ch, K—R1; 18 NxP ch, RxN; 19 Q—Q8 ch forcing mate.

15	....	P—R3!

An important move. It rules out the variations just shown, and in reply to such retreats as 16 Q—Q2 or 16 Q—N3 it makes 16 . . . PxB; 17 NxP, RxR ch; 18 RxR, Q—K2 possible. (With White's Queen on King Knight 5, . . . Q—K2 was impossible.)

16	Q—R4	....

To prevent . . . Q—K2.

16	....	QxN!

This move, ignored or disdained by previous commentators, is apparently Fischer's secret weapon.

White is now a piece down, with another *en prise*; in addition there is a disquieting looseness in his position which augurs badly for him.

If, for example, 17 R—N3 the sequel might be 17 . . . Q—B4; 18 R—N3, PxB and White's attack has petered out.

17	RxBP	....

The position calls for heroic action.

17	....	RxR
18	Q—Q8 ch	....

Or 18 R—KB1, NxP and Black can hold his own.

18	....	N—B1
19	BxR ch	KxB
20	R—KB1 ch	....

Hoping that Black will stumble into 20 . . . K—N1?; 21 RxN ch, K—R2; 22 R—R8 ch, K—N3; 23 Q—K8 ch, K—N4; 24 N—B3 ch and White must win.

20	....	K—N3!

DIAGRAM 106 Position after 20 . . . K—N3!

Black (FISCHER)

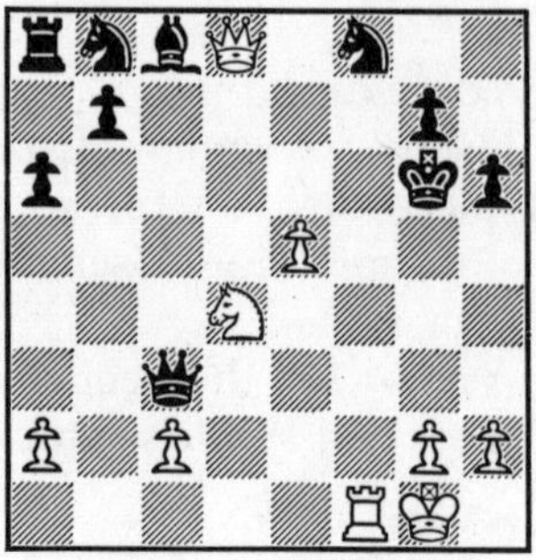

White (BILEK)

21 RxN . . . .

Fischer undoubtedly perceived that after 21 Q—K8 ch, K—R2; 22 RxN (threatening mate) he would have an easy win with 22 . . . Q—K8 ch!; 23 R—B1, Q—K6 ch; 24 R—B2, B—Q2! followed by . . . QxN with two pieces up.

21 . . . . B—Q2!

Preventing Q—K8 ch and also threatening . . . QxN ch.

22 N—B3 . . . .

If 22 R—B6 ch (hoping to draw after 22 . . . PxR?; 23 QxP ch etc.), Black replies 22 . . . K—R2! and White is embarrassed for a good continuation.

22 . . . . Q—K6 ch

Forcing White's reply, for if 23 K—B1??, B—N4 ch is deadly.

23 K—R1 Q—B8 ch

At this point Black had used up only seven minutes on his clock, whereas White had only seven minutes left to make his next 17 moves for the time control.

24	N—N1	QxBP

A pretty variation here is 25 Q—K7 (threatening to draw with 26 Q—B7 ch), QxRP; 26 RxN, RxR; 27 Q—Q6 ch, K—R2; 28 QxR, B—B3; 29 N—B3, Q—R8 ch; 30 N—N1, Q—KB8! forcing mate.

25	R—N8	Q—B7

White was threatening 26 Q—B6 ch etc.

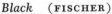

DIAGRAM 107 Position after 25 . . . Q—B7

Black (FISCHER)

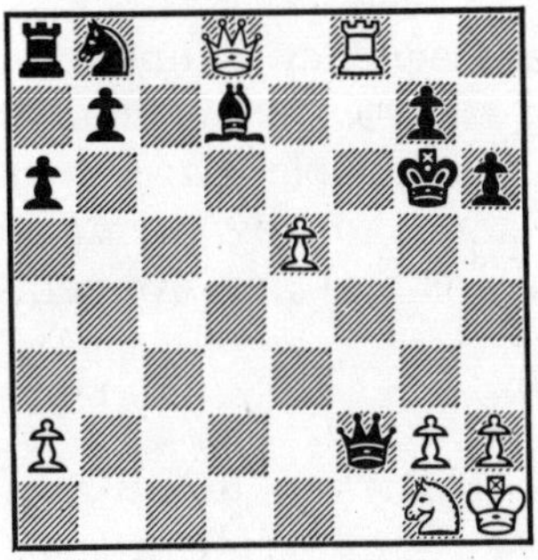

White (BILEK)

White can now prolong the game, though to no useful purpose, with 26 P—KR3 (to free his Knight), B—K3!; 27 R—K8 (or 27 R—B8, N—Q2!), B—B2; 28 R—B8, N—Q2!; 29 QxR, NxR; 30 QxN, QxRP with an easy win for Black.

26	R—B8	QxRP
27	R—B3	K—R2
	Resigns	

White overstepped the time limit here, but he had nothing more to hope for. Thus, after 28 R—KN3, Q—N1! Black frees his Knight for action, while after 28 P—R3,

Q—Q4! the win is only a question of time (29 R—B8, B—B3! or 29 Q—K7, N—B3). A fine example of Fischer's coolness under fire.

54 *SICILIAN DEFENSE*

INTERZONAL TOURNAMENT / STOCKHOLM / 1962

Tie for Second Brilliancy Prize

No reader of this book can have failed to perceive the importance of the Sicilian Defense in Fischer's games. It is his favorite weapon against 1 P—K4 and it has been adopted with great frequency against him when he has the White pieces, with 1 P—K4 as his invariable opening move. It is therefore understandable that he has devoted an enormous amount of study to this opening in the search for significant innovations and improvements.

	White	*Black*
	FISCHER	BOLBOCHAN
1	P—K4	P—QB4
2	N—KB3	P—Q3
3	P—Q4	PxP
4	NxP	N—KB3
5	N—QB3	P—QR3
6	P—KR3!?	....

There are many variations of the Sicilian Defense in which the "bayonet" attack with P—KN4 forms the characteristic feature. But to play this move right in the opening, as implied by White's last move, is enough to make Black very uneasy.

DIAGRAM 108 Position after 6 P—KR3!?

Black (BOLBOCHAN)

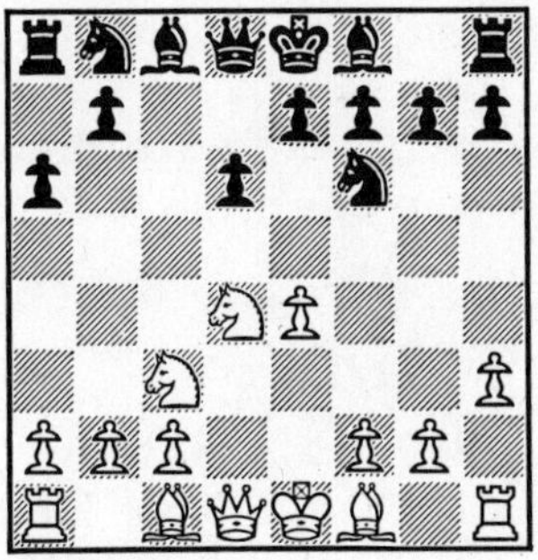

White (FISCHER)

If Black has his wits about him he probably should try 6 . . . P—K4; 7 KN—K2, B—K3; 8 P—KN4, P—Q4. In that case the logical line would be 9 P—N5! NxP; 10 NxN, PxN; 11 QxQ ch, KxQ; 12 N—N3, B—Q4; 13 B—K3 (threatens to win a piece by castling), K—B2; 14 Castles, B—B3; 15 B—N2 and White recovers his Pawn with a promising ending.

6	. . . .	N—B3
7	P—KN4	NxN

Black plays this for lack of any more inspiring idea. The position is, to be sure, difficult to appraise.

8	QxN	P—K4

This move is common to a number of Sicilian variations which share the same characteristic: the Queen Pawn is rendered backward and Black's Q4 square becomes an inviting outpost for White's Knight. This last consideration is all the more threatening since Black's Knight will be driven away from its present square.

9	Q—Q3	B—K2

An earlier game, Gereben-Geller (Budapest, 1952), now continued: 10 B—N2, B—K3; 11 P—N3?, Castles; 12 B—N2, P—QN4; 13 Castles/Q?, P—N5 and Black obtained a powerful attack which earned a brilliancy prize. In the following play, however, Fischer improves substantially on White's conduct of that game.

Incidentally, 9 . . . P—KR3 (to prevent White's next move) can be answered effectively by 10 P—B4.

10	P—N5	N—Q2
11	B—K3!	. . . .

For after 11 . . . BxP; 12 BxB, QxB; 13 QxQP, Q—K2; 14 QxQ ch, KxQ; 15 N—Q5 ch Black has a very bad game: 15 . . . K—Q1; 16 Castles threatening to win at once with 17 B—N6 ch! Or 15 . . . K—Q3; 16 Castles, K—B3; 17 R—N1, P—KN3; 18 R—N3 with the winning threat of R—QB3 ch etc.

11	. . . .	N—B4
12	Q—Q2	B—K3
13	Castles	Castles
14	P—B3	R—B1
15	K—N1	N—Q2

Contemplating the maneuver . . . N—N3—B5. White foresees that he will capture the Knight after . . . N—N3, so he gives his King Knight Pawn additional protection.

16	P—KR4	P—N4
17	B—R3!	. . . .

White wants to eliminate Black's more useful Bishop—and also to intensify his hold on the Q5 square.

17	. . . .	BxB

This capture has been criticized, but after some such alternative as 17 . . . R—K1; 18 N—Q5, B—B1; 19 Q—N2 White would maintain stifling pressure. Or 17 . . . N—N3; 18 BxN, QxB; 19 N—Q5!, Q—Q1 (forced); 20 NxB ch and White wins a Pawn.

18	RxB	N—N3

With a view to . . . N—B5.

19	BxN!	QxB
20	N—Q5	Q—Q1

Black has set a trap: 21 NxB ch, QxN; 22 QxP??, KR—Q1 winning the Queen.

21	P—KB4!	PxP

Else P—B5 strangles him.

22	QxP	Q—Q2

DIAGRAM 109 Position after 22 . . . Q—Q2

Black (BOLBOCHAN)

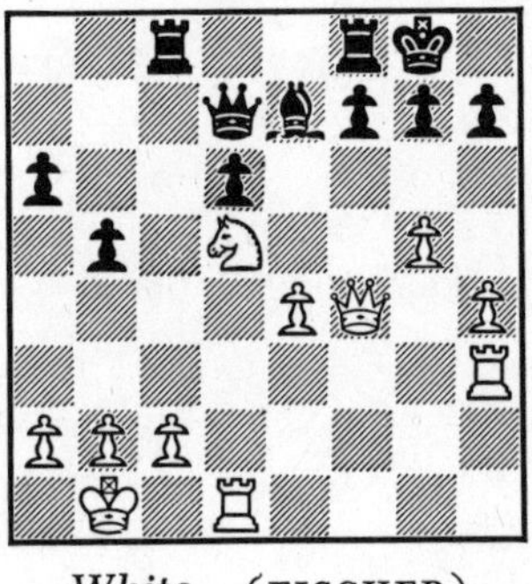

White (FISCHER)

23	Q—B5!	. . . .

An amazingly powerful move which gives Black a wide range of losing moves.

Thus, if 23 . . . QxQ; 24 NxB ch wins a piece. Or if 23 . . . KR—Q1; 24 QxQ, RxQ; 25 N—N6 winning the exchange. Curiously, 23 . . . Q—Q1 allows 24 QxR! etc.

Another possibility: 23 . . . Q—N2; 24 N—B6 ch!, PxN; 25 PxP, BxP; 26 QxB, KR—Q1; 27 R—N3 ch, K—B1; 28

P—K5, P—Q4; 29 P—K6 and wins. Or 24 . . . BxN; 25 PxB, P—N3; 26 Q—N5 (threatens Q—R6), K—R1; 27 P—R5, QxP; 28 QR—R1 and wins, the threat being 29 PxP, QxNP; 30 QxQ (or 30 RxP ch etc.), PxQ; 31 RxP ch, K—N1; 32 R—KN7 mate.

23	....	QR—Q1
24	R—R3!	Q—R2
25	R—QB3!	....

On the immediate 25 N—B6 ch, BxN; 26 PxB Black can hold out with 26 . . . Q—B4. But now White has wiped out this resource, and threatens 27 R—B7 for good measure.

25	....	P—N3

On 25 . . . R—Q2; 26 N—B6 ch is deadly: for example, 26 . . . BxN; 27 PxB, P—N3; 28 Q—N5, K—R1; 29 Q—R6, R—KN1; 30 R—B8! and mate follows.

26	Q—N4	Q—Q2
27	Q—B3	Q—K3
28	R—B7	....

Now 28 . . . R—Q2? is disastrous because of 29 N—B4! winning a Rook.

28	....	QR—K1
29	N—B4	Q—K4
30	R—Q5	Q—R1
31	P—R3!	....

Once again it will prove useful to provide a loophole for the King.

31	....	P—R3

Air!

32	PxP	QxRP
33	P—R5	B—N4

Or 33 . . . P—N4; 34 N—N2 followed by N—K3—B5 with crushing pressure.

34 PxP! ....

For if 34 . . . BxN; 35 PxP ch, RxP; 36 RxR, KxR; 37 R—KB5 ch with an easy win for White.

34 .... PxP

Now it would seem that White must lose a piece. Has he blundered?

DIAGRAM 110 Position after 34 . . . PxP

Black (BOLBOCHAN)

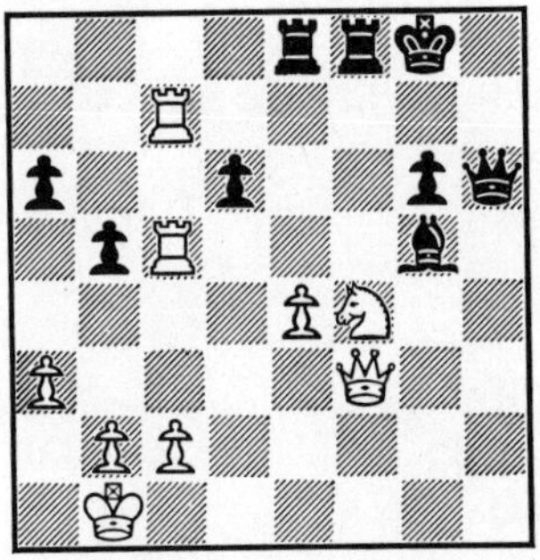

White (FISCHER)

35 Q—QN3!! ....

Beautiful. If Black flees from the discovered check by 35 . . . K—R1 there follows 36 NxP ch!, QxN; 37 RxB!, R—B8 ch; 38 K—R2 (thanks to 31 P—R3!), QxR; 39 Q—KR3 ch and White forces mate.

35 .... RxN

On 35 . . . R—B2; 36 RxB wins out of hand, while if 35 . . . BxN, 36 R—R5 dis ch etc.

36 R—K5 dis ch! ....

The strongest discovered check.

36	....	K—B1
37	RxR ch	Resigns

For if 37 . . . KxR; 38 Q—N8 ch, Q—B1; 39 Q—K6 ch, B—K2; 40 R—B8 mate. A gem of a game.

55 *SICILIAN DEFENSE*

CANDIDATES' TOURNAMENT / CURACAO / 1962

Fischer is generally at his best in hard-fought endings which require nicety of judgment. Here he outplays a former World Champion after a somewhat dubious opening.

	White	*Black*
	FISCHER	TAL
1	P—K4	P—QB4
2	N—KB3	N—QB3
3	P—Q4	PxP
4	NxP	P—K4!?

For a century or more this move was dismissed as a strategic blunder because of the resulting backwardness of Black's Queen Pawn.

It must be noted, however, that earlier games (Morphy-Loewenthal, Match, 1858, and Schlechter–Dr. Lasker, Match, 1910), did not turn out too badly for Black. The former continued 5 NxN, NPxN; 6 B—QB4, N—B3 which leaves Black with a fair game, the proper course doubtless being . . . B—K2 followed by . . . P—Q3. The second game went 5 N—N3, B—N5; 6 B—Q3, P—Q4 with a good game for Black.

5	N—N5	P—QR3
6	N—Q6 ch	BxN
7	QxB	Q—B3!

The new wrinkle. If now 8 QxQ, NxQ; 9 N—B3, P—Q4!; 10 PxP, N—QN5! and Black recovers his Pawn with an excellent game.

8	Q—Q1	Q—N3
9	N—B3	KN—K2
10	P—KR4	....

White hopes to profit from the somewhat awkward position of Black's Queen.

10	....	P—KR4
11	B—KN5	....

DIAGRAM 111 Position after 11 B—KN5

Black (TAL)

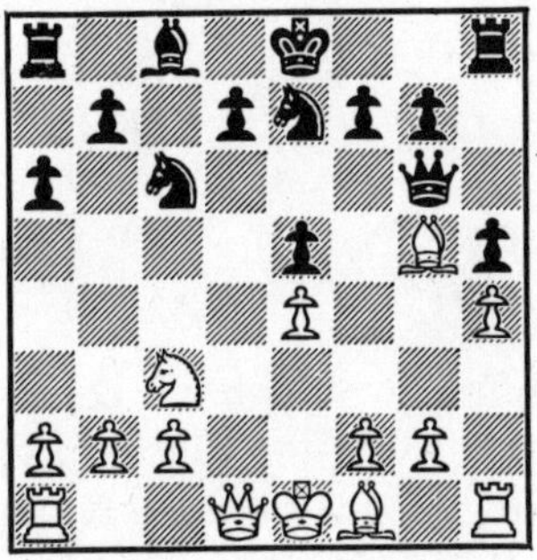

White (FISCHER)

Black's fanciful play looks suspicious, for he is still left with the backward Queen Pawn.

11	....	P—Q4!
12	BxN	....

Or 12 PxP, N—Q5; 13 B—Q3, B—B4 and Black has strong play for the Pawn.

12	....	P—Q5!
13	B—KN5	PxN
14	PxP	QxP ch

Suddenly it is White who has weak Pawns, while Black is rid of his.

15	B—K2	P—B3

Not 15 . . . QxNP??; 16 B—B3 trapping Black's Queen.

16	B—K3	B—N5

On 16 . . . QxNP; 17 BxKRP ch gives White a considerable advantage, as 17 . . . P—KN3 will not do because of 18 B—B3 trapping Black's Queen again.

17	Q—Q3!	QxQ

Though this straightens out White's Pawns, Black has no choice (17 . . . QxP?; 18 Q—N6 ch and White has a winning attack).

18	PxQ	BxB
19	KxB	Castles/Q
20	QR—Q1	N—K2
21	P—Q4	N—Q4
22	R—QB1	KR—K1
23	KR—Q1	. . . .

This suggests that it would have been more accurate to play 20 KR—Q1. In any event Black has the better ending and could maintain his positional advantage with 23 . . . PxP; 24 PxP dis ch, K—N1 etc.

23	. . . .	P—B4!?

Promising, but also risky.

24	B—N5!	. . . .

Fischer seizes the proffered opportunity.

24	. . . .	R—Q2

Or 24 . . . PxP dis ch; 25 K—B3 and White recovers the Pawn.

25	PxP	RxP ch
26	K—B3	R—K5

27	R—Q3	R—QB5
28	R/B1—Q1!	....

Played with fine insight into the position. Instead of trying to hold on to the weakling, Fischer surrenders it at once, with a view to counterattacking on the other wing. From now on White has a standing threat eventually to play K—B4—N5 under propitious circumstances.

28	....	RxBP
29	RxR	NxR
30	R—QB1!	....

This leads to difficult play, though Black's best try seems 30 . . . R—Q6 ch; 31 K—B4, K—Q2! (not 31 . . . P—KN3??; 32 B—B6) and now 32 R—B2 can be answered by 32 . . . K—K3 and 32 KxP by 32 . . . NxP.

DIAGRAM 112 Position after 30 R—QB1!

Black (TAL)

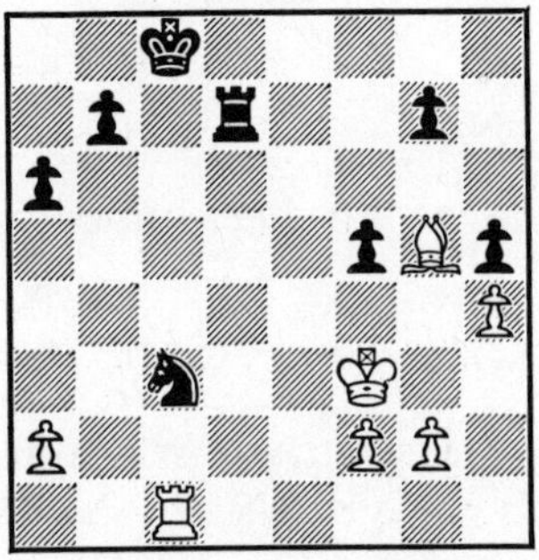

White (FISCHER)

30	....	R—QB2?
31	B—B4!	R—B3
32	B—K5!	N—Q4!

After 32 . . . NxP; 33 RxR ch, PxR; 34 BxP the ending may be a win for White (despite his Pawn down) as in this variation given by Kmoch: 34 . . . K—Q2; 35 K—B4, K—K3; 36 K—N5, P—R4; 37 KxRP, P—R5; 38 K—N6 and White wins the ending.

33	R—Q1!	. . . .

But here after 33 RxR ch, PxR; 34 BxP, K—Q2 White would be less well off because his King cannot play to KB4.

33	. . . .	N—B3

Black is losing the thread of the game. He could still hold with 33 . . . K—Q2!; 34 RxN ch, K—K3; 35 R—R5, P—QN3 or 34 BxP, K—K3.

34	K—B4!	P—KN3
35	P—B3	N—Q2
36	B—Q6	R—B7
37	P—N3!	. . . .

White is satisfied that after 37 . . . RxP; 38 K—N5 followed by 39 KxNP and 40 KxRP his passed King Rook Pawn will win for him, the Bishop being very superior in this type of ending with passed Pawns on opposite wings.

37	. . . .	R—K7
38	K—N5	R—K3

A flimsy defense, as Fischer immediately demonstrates.

39	B—B4	N—B1
40	R—Q6!	P—R4!

Apparently with this variation in mind: 41 RxR, NxR ch; 42 KxNP, NxB ch; 43 PxN, P—N4; 44 KxBP!, P—N5; 45 K—K4!, P—R5; 46 K—Q4, K—Q2; 47 K—B4, P—N6; 48 PxP, PxP; 49 KxP, K—K3; 50 K—B3, K—B4; 51 K—Q3, KxP; 52 K—K2, K—N6 (Kmoch) and the ending is a draw.

DIAGRAM 113 Position after 40 . . . P—R4!

Black (TAL)

White (FISCHER)

41	K—R6!	R—K7
42	R—Q2	R—K2
43	B—Q6	R—R2 ch
44	K—N5	R—KB2
45	R—QN2!!	. . . .

Beautiful play. Any move of a Black piece loses a Pawn—to begin with. And after 45 . . . P—R5; 46 P—R3! Black remains in the same predicament.

45	. . . .	P—B5
46	BxP	R—B4 ch
47	K—R6	P—N4
48	B—Q6!	. . . .

Forestalling 48 . . . K—Q2.

48	. . . .	P—N5

Or 48 . . . RxP; 49 RxP and White wins with ease.

49	P—N4!	RxP
50	P—N5!	. . . .

Now White intends BxN followed by the capture of both Black King-side Pawns. White's play is very fine hereabouts.

50	....	N—K3
51	KxP	R—Q6
52	B—K5	R—K6
53	K—B5	N—B1

Hoping for 54 P—N6?, NxP etc.

54	R—N2!	R—KB6 ch
55	B—B4	K—Q2
56	P—N6	N—K3
57	P—N7!	RxB ch
58	K—K5	R—B1
59	PxR/Q	NxQ
60	K—Q5	P—R5
61	R—N7 ch	K—K1
62	K—Q6	P—N6
63	P—R3!	Resigns

If 63 . . . K—Q1; 64 R—QR7 (threatening mate), K—K1; 65 RxP winning easily. A masterly ending.

56 *RUY LOPEZ*

CANDIDATES' TOURNAMENT / CURAÇAO / 1962

To defeat a great tactician like Keres with his own weapons is a feat which sets off Fischer's outstanding capabilities in the best light.

	White	*Black*
	FISCHER	KERES
1	P—K4	P—K4
2	N—KB3	N—QB3
3	B—N5	P—QR3
4	B—R4	N—B3
5	Castles	B—K2
6	R—K1	P—QN4

7	B—N3	P—Q3
8	P—B3	Castles
9	P—KR3	N—QR4
10	B—B2	P—B4
11	P—Q4	....

In the 1920's this was known as the "Stereotyped Variation," because it was thought that the last word had been said on the subject. Yet the modern masters have continued to find interesting novelties.

DIAGRAM 114 Position after 11 P—Q4

Black (KERES)

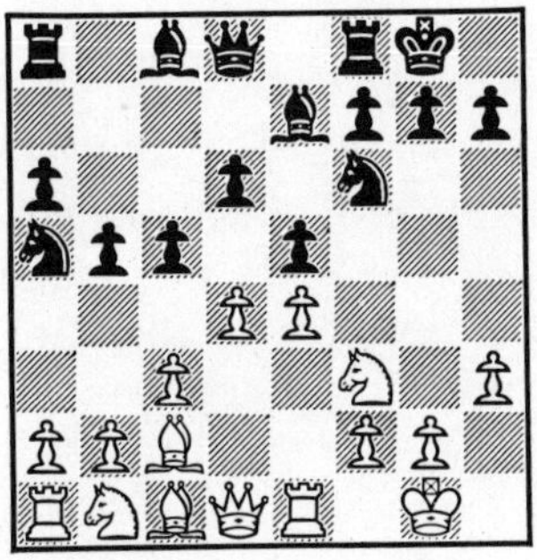

White (FISCHER)

11	....	N—Q2

This Knight is headed for QN3, but the notion of planting both Knights on the Queen-side is somewhat questionable, in view of the rather unprotected state of Black's King-side later on.

12	PxBP	PxP
13	QN—Q2	Q—B2
14	N—B1	N—N3
15	N—K3	R—Q1
16	Q—K2	B—K3

The idea of exchanging Pawns and then striving for N—Q5 is a favorite with Fischer.

17 N—Q5!? ....

This confronts Black with difficult problems. He can try to win a Pawn with 17 . . . BxN; 18 PxB, P—B3; but then comes 19 Q—K4, P—N3; 20 N—R4 (threatening NxP), P—B4; 21 NxBP, PxN; 22 QxBP, B—B1; 23 RxP with a tremendous attack.

17 .... NxN

Certainly playable, but then the question arises: why move the Knight three times in order to carry out an exchange that could just as well have been played with the Knight at KB3?!

18	PxN	BxQP
19	NxP	....

To the uninitiated eye the position looks fairly even. But Fischer is well aware that Black's denuded King-side, bereft of protection by the absence of the King Knight, may be vulnerable to sharp attack. For example, White threatens 20 B—B4, Q—N3; 21 NxP.

19 .... R—R2

This creates difficulties because Black's first rank turns out to be weak in some variations. But even after 19 . . . B—B1; 20 Q—Q3, P—N3; 21 Q—N3! White would have good attacking chances.

20	B—B4	Q—N3
21	QR—Q1!	....

Now White threatens 22 RxB!, RxR; 23 Q—K4 and wins.

DIAGRAM 115 Position after 21 QR—Q1!

Black (KERES)

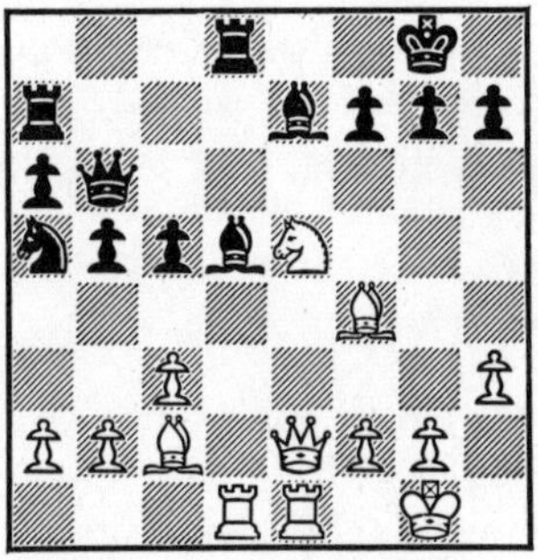

White (FISCHER)

21 .... P—N3

Kmoch gives an exceedingly complicated variation after 21 . . . BxRP: 22 RxR ch, QxR (if 22 . . . BxR?; 23 N—B4! wins); 23 P—QN4!, PxP; 24 PxP, BxP; 25 Q—K4!, BxR; 26 QxP ch, K—B1; 27 Q—R8 ch, K—K2; 28 N—N6 ch, K—Q2 best; 29 B—K3; 30 BxB ch, PxB; 31 QxP ch, K—K1; 32 Q—B8 ch, K—Q2; 33 Q—B7 ch, K—B1; 34 QxR and wins!

22 N—N4! ....

Now White threatens 23 Q—K5!, P—B3; 24 QxKB!, RxQ; 25 RxR and there is no good defense to the threat of B—B7, for example 25 . . . B—N2; 26 RxR ch, QxR; 27 R—Q7!, Q—KB1; 28 B—R6 etc.

22 .... N—B5

If instead 22 . . . B—B5 (or 22 . . . BxRP); 23 Q—K5, P—B3; 24 QxB!, RxQ; 25 RxR/K7, RxR ch; 26 BxR and wins. The primary threat is 27 B—B7 and if Black plays 27 . . . N—B3 there follows 28 NxP ch, K—B1; 29 N—Q7 ch and wins. Or 27 . . . N—N2; 28 B—B7!, Q—R2 (if 28 . . . . Q—B3; 29 B—B3, B—Q4; 30 BxB ch, QxB; 31 NxP ch winning the Queen); 29 NxP ch, K—B1; 30 R—Q7! and Black has no defense.

23 B—R6! ....

The attack is shaping up. A curious variation here is 23 . . . NxP?; 24 RxB!, RxR; 25 B—K4, R—R4; 26 QxN, P—B4; 27 B—Q5 ch, K—R1; 28 P—QB4 dis ch and wins.

23 .... B—K3
24 B—N3! ....

White threatens 25 RxR ch, QxR; 26 BxN, BxB; 27 N—B6 ch, K—R1 (if 27 . . . BxN; 28 Q—K8 ch forces mate) 28 Q—K5! and Black is helpless against the coming discovered check.

DIAGRAM 116 Position after 24 B—N3!

Black (KERES)

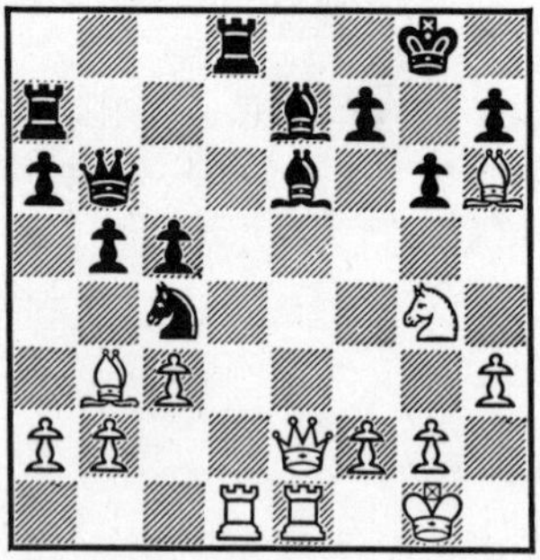

White (FISCHER)

24 .... Q—N1

Here the annotators have recommended 24 . . . RxR; 25 RxR, Q—N1 as sufficient to hold the position. But then after 26 BxN, BxB; 27 Q—K5!, QxQ; 28 NxQ White threatens 29 N—B6, R—B2; 30 NxB ch, RxN; 31 R—Q8 ch forcing mate. Consequently, after 28 NxQ Black must play some such move as 28 . . . P—B3 allowing 29 NxB. Given the weakness of Black's Pawns after 29 . . . PxN Black's loss in the endgame is quite certain.

25	RxR ch!	BxR

Or 25 . . . QxR; 26 BxN, BxB; 27 N—B6 ch and wins. Or 26 . . . PxB; 27 Q—K5 and wins.

26	BxN	PxB

The alternative 26 . . . BxB allows mate on the move.

27	QxP!	. . . .

The obvious but pretty point of White's attacking play. Because he now threatens 28 RxB there is no time for 27 . . . QxP.

27	. . . .	Q—Q3
28	Q—R4	. . . .

Threatening mate. Instead of being content with his material gain, White continues to play aggressively.

28	. . . .	Q—K2
29	N—B6 ch!	K—R1

And not 29 . . . QxN??; 30 Q—K8 mate.

30	N—Q5	Q—Q2
31	Q—K4!	. . . .

Threatening 32 Q—K5 ch, K—N1; 33 N—B6 ch, BxN; 34 QxB ch and mate next move.

31	. . . .	Q—Q3

Of course if 31 . . . QxN?; 32 QxQ and Black cannot retake.

32	N—B4	. . . .

Now White wins a second Pawn (32 . . . B—Q2; 33 Q—K8 ch forcing mate).

32	....	R—K2
33	B—N5!	R—K1
34	BxB	RxB
35	NxB	QxN

Or 35 . . . R—K1; 36 Q—K5 ch, QxQ; 37 RxQ, PxN; 38 RxBP with two Pawns up (or 37 . . . RxN; 38 RxR and the King and Pawn ending is an easy win).

36	QxQ	PxQ
37	RxP	R—Q ch
38	K—R2	R—Q7
39	R—N6!	RxBP
40	R—N7!	....

To keep Black's King out.

40	....	R—B3
41	K—N3	Resigns

A trifle prematurely, perhaps, but White has many ways to win, for example P—QR4—5 followed by R—N6. A very enjoyable game.

794.1 R367G
REINFELD, FRED.
Great games by chess prodigies.
5707

Date Due

APR 14 '67			
APR 6 '72			
NOV 8 '72			
NOV 21 '72			
APR 19 '80			
APR 24 '89			
MAY 31 '89			